MAPPING
Your
CAREER

MAPPING *Your* CAREER

The book that can help you find
the job you want, and create
the career you are meant for

The Crisp Editors
Foreword by
Richard N. Bolles

CRISP.
Learning
Menlo Park, California

Mapping Your Career

The Crisp Editors

Material in this book has been reprinted or adapted, with permission, from the following works published by Crisp Publications:

Attitude: Your Most Priceless Possession by Elwood Chapman
I Got the Job by Elwood Chapman
Job Search that Works by Richard Lamplugh
Strategic Resumes by Marci Mahoney
Preparing for Your Interview by Diane Berk
Jobsearch.net by Carrie Straub

Additional material in this book has been reprinted or adapted from training materials developed by Cuyahoga Community College Career Place, and is used with their permission.

Cover Design: **FifthStreet Design**

© 2002 Crisp Publications, Inc.
Printed in the United States of America by Von Hoffmann Graphics, Inc.

CrispLearning.com

01 02 03 04   10 9 8 7 6 5 4 3 2 1

Library of Congress Catalog Card Number 2001093621
The Crisp Editors
Mapping Your Career
ISBN 1-56052-646-7

Foreword

Of the making of many books about careers there is no end, and much reading of them is a weariness to the flesh. Well, that isn't exactly the way Ecclesiastes wrote it, but it serves to introduce this book. Mostly they are a weariness to the flesh because they make the subject too complicated, too complex, and they spend too long saying what they want to say.

The reader ends up not only weary but also perplexed. The people who are likely to feel the most perplexed (and the least confident) are those just starting out—whether it be in school, or on their first or second job, or any other time when they are uncertain about what direction to take with their lives. The reader hungers for simplicity, and help which doesn't make a subject more difficult than it needs to be.

That's what is appealing about this book. It approaches the world of work, the job search, and career development simply, treating it as a journey. And for a journey, you need a map.

The map-makers who created this book come from a career center at a small community college in Ohio. They were able to put something together, by way of a map, that is simple and suited to the college student. This is, after all, the population they are most experienced in working with.

Such a person just starting out, or making a serious life-change, can come back to this workbook time and again, as you would with a map, to check direction and make needed changes. What it also offers, in addition to a map, are the navigation tools that come in handy when detours and caution signs appear. These include an awareness of one's most useful and enjoyed skills; a measure of one's values and goals; an understanding of the possibilities in change; and a down-to-earth appreciation of the serious preparation and work it takes to go after what one really wants.

The job search, thence career change, plus a consideration of what life can become, are parts of the journey we all must take. It is handy to have a guidebook like MAPPING YOUR CAREER at one's elbow, as that journey unfolds.

Richard N. Bolles
Author, *What Color Is Your Parachute?*
March 2001

Contents

INTRODUCTION

Getting Started

"Who are You?" said the Caterpillar.
"I – I hardly know, Sir, just at present – at least I know who I was when I got up this morning, but I think I must have been changed several times since then."

Alice, Adventures in Wonderland, by Lewis Carroll
Pseudonym of Charles Lutwidge Dodgson
English writer, mathematician, and amateur photographer
1832–1898

Imagine That!

Henry Ford once said, "If you think you can or think you can't, you're right."

Whatever you believe will come to be. If you believe you will become employed, you will. That's because all your efforts will be focused on finding a job, rather than on seeing yourself as unemployable.

When you think about the positive goals instead of the negative problems, you're being optimistic. Optimism can be one of the first things to go when you face life's problems. But optimism is unquestionably the best friend you will ever have when you're facing challenges. Focus on the possibilities of tomorrow, not the problems of today.

Sit down now. Imagine yourself in the job you want. See yourself doing it well. Now, run the memory tape backwards. Picture your job interview and how well it went. Listen to how well you communicated. Go back further. Imagine yourself calling on employers every day. See how this produced the interview that turned into your new job. Keep going back. See yourself using possibility thinking to arrive at several job goals. Notice the difference. Once you would never have thought of yourself in these jobs. But right now, they feel just fine.

Perhaps you have a lot of time on your hands these days. Use this extra time. Do some imagining. You'll see a huge difference in your job search if you spend undisturbed time every day visualizing your *successful* job search. You can use this visualizing as the first step in a four-step approach to finding the job you want.

1 **Imagine.** Imagine yourself in the job you want. Take your mind off unemployment. Think of employment. Picture yourself accepting a job offer.

2 **Commit.** Commit to yourself and other positive people about your goal and how you'll achieve it. Nothing can stop a totally committed person. Your train of life may be delayed, but it won't be derailed.

3 **Affirm.** Do positive self-talk. Give yourself a pat on the back when you do well at locating employers, preparing for an interview, or other steps in your job search. Be your own cheerleader.

4 **Persist.** Keep after your job goal. Decide that you WILL find the job you want. Decide that you do not accept being unemployed as anything more than it is—a short-term situation.

Change-Readiness:
An Adaptive Skill

Change-readiness will be your best friend when you find yourself needing or wanting to make a move. It is a state of mind that is geared to the benefits of new events. It is a resolve to do whatever may be required to achieve a better situation.

When you have change-readiness, you can absorb the pressures of disruptive or displacing outside factors. You can move ahead with your life. When you have change-readiness, you are attuned to your instincts around what you need to do to earn a living and you can create your right livelihood.

Catalysts for change can be external or internal. For the change-ready person, it does not matter. What matters is his or her core disposition to relate to change, to see it as a vehicle for important personal and career development.

On Developing Change-Readiness

Developing change-readiness may mean doing some emotional homework. It may mean recognizing the pull of the familiar, of the status quo, and getting in touch with your motivation for a more meaningful alternative. It may mean developing a shield against wavering thoughts about your personal potential and outside influences that discourage your move.

You may want to look at your support systems, the people in your life who believe in you and want you to succeed. These are the people who will listen to you, talk with you frankly, cheer you on, and in various other ways be invaluable resources.

Finally, you may want to take a look at what you can do to build in flexibility for taking quick and effective action in new career initiatives. How clear are you about realistic and attractive options? How prepared are you to discuss opportunities with new employers?

Food for Thought

> *"You must do the thing you think you cannot do."*
>
> Eleanor Roosevelt
> American humanitarian and wife of President Franklin D. Roosevelt
> 1884–1962

 A CHANGE-READINESS QUIZ

Place a check on the scale below for each of the following statements, at the point that best describes how you relate to change:

1. I find change to be basically:

   Disruptive _____ Stimulating

2. I see change as:

   Crisis _____ Opportunity

3. I make changes:

   When necessary _____When possible

4. I handle change:

   With difficulty _____ With ease

Circle the response that describes your current career situation:

5. I have a "Plan A" for my next career move.   Yes   No

6. I have a "Plan B" for my next career move.   Yes   No

7. I have at least three months of income saved as
   a buffer against unemployment.   Yes   No

8. I have some realistic ideas about interim jobs
   I could do, if I need to.   Yes   No

Complete the following unfinished sentences:

• A change I want to make in my employment situation is:

   _____

• Factors I have going for me in making this change include:

   _____

• Additional things I can do to enhance my change-readiness are:

   _____

Managing Change by Managing Your Career

In the midst of changing workplace conditions, there is a resource for pathfinding—a very powerful and reliable resource. It is a way for you to find direction when there are no external signs and signals telling you where to go and when to stop and go.

Career Management: Concept, Skills and Commitment

The Career Management Concept

The core concept in career management is that you have the freedom and the responsibility to manage your own career. No one else can do it for you. No one else will do it for you. And no one else will care as much about your career.

When managing your career becomes a self-directed process, you gain a great deal of control over your working life. You take ownership of realizing your personal potential. You become a stakeholder in developing ways to earn a living, no matter what options close down for you along the way.

Career Management Skills

Career management means identifying what you have to offer and what you want to do. It means defining goals that are consistent with your greatest strengths and interests, connected to needs in the marketplace. It means scouting out opportunity that is often in obscure and unexpected places, and communicating effectively with "...people who can help leverage you for a position or hire you."

Once selected for a new job or a new assignment, career management means delivering peak performance, staying attuned constantly to adding value, practicing learning as a way of life, and building and maintaining strong relationships with your co-workers, colleagues and customers.

Career Management Commitment

Your commitment to managing your career will be the single most important factor in your success. It will get you going and keep you going when times are hard. It will help you take horizon-broadening risks. It will drive every initiative you make, and motivate employers to invest in themselves by investing in you.

Research

Put on your library hat; you're going to do some research. What exactly do you need to find out?

Find books that describe jobs. Professionals you are working with will have some. The library will have others. These two are good ones:

The *Occupational Outlook Handbook*–describes hundreds of jobs available in the United States today.

The *Dictionary of Occupational Titles*–describes what workers do in thousands of jobs.

Statewide occupation information–distributed by a state agency–describes many jobs available in your state.

These excellent guides will give you background for understanding almost any job: new trends in a particular job or industry, what skills will suit a particular job, what kind of experience an employer looks for, what the future may bring in a particular field.

Most of the information that you need can also be found on the Internet.

Research helps you get interviews and job offers more quickly. Time spent on research will *save you time* in returning to work. This means you start seeing a paycheck sooner. So, research time is not only well spent–*it pays for itself.*

Become an Expert

Learn about the job you are seeking. Employers look for three things:

Skills

These are abilities you have that you've gained through life or work. Some skills are direct, like knowing how to set up and operate the production drill press. Others are transferable. For example, Luella wants to be a receptionist, something she's never done before. However, she has worked as a sales clerk, so she knows how to handle cash and has operated an adding machine. She has skills that will help her be a good receptionist.

Attitude

This is what's inside you that makes you use your skills to produce results. Every employer is looking for a "good attitude," but only you, the worker, can develop it. For example, Mel, an auto parts counter worker, is willing to take his lunch break a half hour later if there is a noontime rush of customers.

Results

These are produced when you use your skills to work more quickly, easily, cheaply, or efficiently. For example, Roberta, a sales route driver, increased the size of her route from 50 to 100 customers. A potential employer will think, "If she did that for the other company, she will do it for me too."

Food for Thought

> "Each of us brings to our job, whatever it is, our lifetime of experience and our values."
>
> Sandra Day O'Conner
> U.S. Supereme Court Judge
> 1930–

You can find out about the skills, attitude, and results employers look for in several ways:

- **Remember.**
  Think about your past experiences with the kind of job you are now seeking. Write down what you remember.

- **Research.**
  Use some of the readily available books that describe jobs in detail.

- **Conduct informational interviews.**
  Talk to people who do the job or who hire others to do it.

Make Your Choice Now!

Characteristics of successful job-seekers

- Those who remain positive about the challenge.

- Applicants who stay with a system that utilizes recognized job-finding techniques.

- Those who plan their work and work their plan.

- Those who use "networking" as their primary prospecting strategy.

- Those who study and understand the dynamics of a tight job market.

- Those who succeed in all aspects of the job-finding process.

- Those who set goals.

- Add your own ideas here:

  _____

  _____

  _____

  _____

Characteristics of unsuccessful job-seekers

- Those who discourage easily and start looking for excuses.

- Job-seekers who do not bother to research firms ahead of interviews.

- Those who decide making professional use of the telephone is too much trouble.

- Applicants who refuse to devote at least 50% of their job-hunting time to prospecting.

- Those who underestimate the personal contribution to productivity they can make.

- Those who downgrade the importance of keeping a positive attitude.

- Add your own ideas here:

  _____

  _____

  _____

  _____

> A good job-finding process does not just produce a job—it produces the best possible job within the geographical area selected.

 PRELIMINARY QUESTIONS

Write your answers below.

Geographic area in which I would accept a job with enthusiasm: (A specific part of the city? Another city? Another state? Another country?)

Few things are worse than living in a geographical area where you (or family members) are unhappy. When it comes to answering this question, be true to yourself and your future.

_____

_____

Three positions for which I am presently qualified:

Although it is much better to reach for a job that forces you to live up to your potential than accept one that is beneath your skills, it is still an exercise in futility to apply for a job where the qualifications are so rigid you are not a realistic candidate.

_____

_____

Constraints that I have: (shift work, length of commute, size of company, etc.)

Some job-seekers accept a position knowing the situation is untenable. When they do this, they are not being true to the prospective employer or their future.

_____

_____

Beginning compensation that would be acceptable: (including benefits)

Few events are more disturbing than to accept a job in desperation and then learn later that the job you really wanted was available but you were already working and not in a position to compete for it.

_____

_____

Rate Yourself

"One of the greatest pieces of economic wisdom is to know what you do not know."

John Kenneth Galbraith
American economist and public official
1908–

RATING YOURSELF IN TWELVE CATEGORIES

This exercise is designed to provide you with special insights regarding your techniques and strategies as a job-finder and job-winner. Once you discover your strengths and weaknesses you will be in a better position to start your search. Almost everyone can benefit.

- If you feel secure but unhappy in your present position and seek a different, more enjoyable one, you will learn about the 12 steps involved in making such a move.

- If you anticipate being thrown into the labor market in the near future, you can isolate weaknesses ahead of time, make corrections, and be better prepared should the time come.

- If you are already unemployed, this exercise will assist you in reviewing your present strategy and make immediate improvements.

- If you will soon graduate from college and you need to prepare for your first interviews.

- If you are still in school and seek a part-time job.

- If you will soon retire and want to work part-time to keep involved and supplement your income.

There are two sections to the exercise. FIRST, you rate yourself in the 12 categories that are normally a part of the job-seeking process. SECOND, you construct a VISUAL PROFILE that will point out your current strengths and weaknesses. Please read the material and then make the most honest evaluation possible. You do this when you circle the appropriate number from 1 to 10.

- If you circle the number 1, 2, or 3, you are saying you have limited knowledge and experience in this area and need substantial help.

- If you circle the number 4, 5, 6, or 7, you are telling yourself that considerable improvement is needed.

- If you circle an 8, 9, or 10, you are giving yourself a signal you need only a little improvement in this category.

Please be as honest with yourself as possible. Keep in mind that most people rate themselves high in a few areas and low in a few others. Take your time as it will be from these ratings that you will build your profile and plan your strategy.

1 Attitude

As Tom Jackson, author of *Guerilla Tactics in The Job Market* has well-observed, the job-hunting process may best be described as NO NO NO NO NO NO NO NO NO NO NO NO NO NO NO NO NO NO NO NO NO NO NO NO NO NO YES. Hearing a few "no's" and getting a few rejections is usually a part of job-finding. What is your attitude toward this aspect of the job-search process? Can you take rejections and bounce back?

What about your ability to transmit a positive work attitude during interviews? Does your voice say you are anxious to contribute while your attitude says you are not?

Can you interpret the entire job-search process as a "game" or do you hate the prospects before you get started?

If you have a highly positive attitude toward conducting a professional job search, give yourself 2 points. If you are positive about using every possible resource to set up interviews, give yourself another 2 points. If you are willing to upgrade your skills *as you search for a job* give yourself 2 additional points. If you think you can maintain a positive attitude over a long stretch of time, increase your total to 9 or 10 points.

Keep in mind that in any job search, a positive attitude can be your most priceless possession. It is your most valuable personality characteristic. Please rate yourself as high as you can realistically justify.

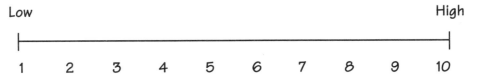

Low   High

1   2   3   4   5   6   7   8   9   10

2 Prospecting

An employer is qualified as a true prospect when he has an opening for which you qualify and is willing to give you an interview. *Prospecting is how you find such employers.* You see unemployed people checking want ads in newspapers and trade journals, visiting placement agencies, and many other prospecting techniques.

Each job search requires a tailored prospecting system. Such a system involves extensive research to identify organizations that could utilize your skills and targeting those for which you would like to work. Some prospecting ideas can be gained from reading books or interviewing those who found jobs in your area ahead of you. Other prospecting techniques will come from experience.

In most situations, people spend more time finding prospects than they do preparing for and going through interviews. One reason for this is that 25% of all jobs are with smaller firms that are more difficult to find. A good system reaches deeply into all segments of the employment market–including all government agencies.

If you have already designed a system that produces two or more qualified prospects per week, give yourself a high grade. If you are confident (through experience) that you can develop such a system, give yourself a score between a 4 and 6. If you have apprehensions about your skill in finding prospects, give yourself a 3 or under.

Low   High

| 1 | 2 | 3 | 4 | 5 | 6 | 7 | 8 | 9 | 10 |

3 Networking

Networking is building a series of strong relationships with people who are in a key position to help you find and win a position where you could reach your potential. Networking can create a chain of events that will lead you to qualified prospects. The players in any system are key people who are in a position to know others who might be interested in your services. Often they are respected people already well-known in your specific field (college professors, consultants, Directors of Human Resource departments). The best way to meet new people who can become part of your networking chain is to join a trade group and attend meetings.

In contacting such people, it is important that you do not communicate you are desperate to get a job, but, rather, you would like suggestions and advice. It is also vital that any relationship created be mutually rewarding—that is, anyone who helps you should enjoy the satisfaction of being a mentor.

Getting the right job is more a matter of good networking than luck. It is *through* networking that you are more apt to wind up at the right place at the right time.

Give yourself a high grade only if you understand the full implications of networking and already have a system in operation. Give yourself an average score if you see the possibilities in networking and have the confidence to initiate a system starting today. If you don't understand networking and it leaves you frustrated, give yourself a low score.

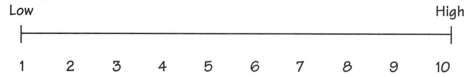

Low   High

| 1 | 2 | 3 | 4 | 5 | 6 | 7 | 8 | 9 | 10 |

4 Telephone Skills

The telephone is the serious job hunter's best friend. Not only can it help you find prospects, the telephone can help you get interview appointments. Used effectively, it can make your job search easier and more effective.

Telemarketing yourself involves such techniques as developing your best voice, accepting rebuffs without getting discouraged, being extra pleasant to switchboard operators, receptionists, and secretaries so you can *get through* to the key people, presenting yourself in such a way that people want to give you an interview, and being persistent.

People who are afraid to make skillful use of the telephone in their job search should circle a low number; those who have confidence to use the telephone but have yet to learn telemarketing techniques should circle a middle number; those who already consider themselves telemarketing experts and are anxious to market themselves should circle a high number.

Low   High

1   2   3   4   5   6   7   8   9   10

5 Internet and Electronic Search

Researching companies, writing resumés that will have high impact when sent over the Internet, and searching for potential jobs using the Internet are now becoming common practices.

Your ability to use the Internet or your comfort with using technology and learning how to use the Internet in your job search will limit potential job leads and access to companies that have job openings.

If you have never used the Internet or are not comfortable using technology in your job search, give yourself a 3 or under. If you are comfortable with technology, know how to use a computer but not very knowledgeable about the Internet, give yourself a 6 or under. If you already use the Internet but need to know about job searching on the Internet, give yourself a higher grade.

Low   High

1   2   3   4   5   6   7   8   9   10

6 Resumé Preparation

A resumé is usually a one-or two-page history of your achievements, education, and characteristics that qualify you for the position you seek. Resumés are designed primarily to gain interviews, but they have many additional uses. Experts claim a resumé should be tailored to the specific job under consideration. Are you already an expert at resumé preparation or should you find a book on the subject or work with a professional?

And don't forget the right letter should accompany your resumé. Models can usually be found in books that deal with resumé preparation.

If you recognize you are weak in this area and need a professional to help you prepare and edit a resumé that will produce interviews, give yourself a 3 or under; if you can do one following instructions in a book, give yourself a 6 or under; if you have recently prepared a resumé that has produced excellent results, give yourself a higher grade.

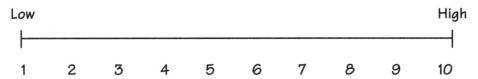

Low   High

1   2   3   4   5   6   7   8   9   10

7 Interview Preparation and Techniques

All 12 steps within the job-winning process are important. The face-to-face interview is critical. How you prepare for it can be as important as the way you perform once it happens. Are you following an exercise program so you appear healthy, eager, and willing to contribute to the productivity level expected by your future employer? Once you get an interview appointment, do you research the background of the firm in preparation for the questioning that usually takes place? Can you answer questions like: What do you know about us? Why did you select us over other firms? Can you name the President of our company? Why did you leave your last employer? What is your career objective? What are your weaknesses? What are your salary expectations? Keep in mind that few employers are interested in "wishy-washy" applicants who cannot provide decisive answers.

There are a number of techniques that need to be mastered, if one wishes an employment interview to turn out successfully. Keeping eye contact when answering questions, injecting humor when the situation calls for it, and asking questions of your own are all recommended. The overriding technique is to *be yourself* and transmit a willingness to learn, be flexible, and adapt to the new environment. On many college campuses these days students are encouraged to do hypothetical interviews which can be rated by other students and the instructor. Assume that you prepared for a hypothetical interview, put it on video, and then sit back and rate yourself.

Rate yourself on the state of readiness you anticipate you will be in when interviews take place. Will you really have done your homework?

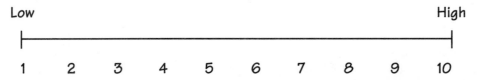

Low   High

1   2   3   4   5   6   7   8   9   10

8 Looking Your Best

What kind of a first impression would you make under the stress of a job interview? Would you be wearing clothes appropriate for the position for which you are applying? For example, a conservative dress or suit might communicate the best image when being interviewed for a position with a financial institution, where something more flamboyant would be appropriate when applying for a position with a media organization. Neatness, cleanliness, use of cosmetics and hairstyle all contribute to the image communicated.

Employers are prohibited from taking race, sex, age, and physical disabilities into consideration, but what you wear and how you have prepared yourself can influence whether you are accepted or rejected. Please circle where you think you would fall in this sensitive area.

9 Skill Upgrading

Employers often require specific skill or competency performance in certain positions. Aptitudes, talents, and personality characteristics often play an important role. In some areas, for example clerical and mechanical, proof of performance levels is often requested. Today, because of technological advancements and continuous upgrading, skills need to be maintained and improved to stay competitive in the labor market.

If you feel you are *fully* competent in all of the skills required in the position for which you are applying, give yourself a high score. If you feel you are *moderately* prepared, rate yourself somewhere in the middle. If you are seeking a job knowing your skills are inferior, give yourself a low grade and do something to improve them immediately.

10 Utilizing Support Services

Both prospecting and networking involve making the maximum use of all available support services. Colleges provide outstanding support services to their students both before and after graduation—yet some students do not take advantage of the help they can provide. The same is true with private employment agencies and government-operated Human Resource departments. In some communities it is possible to join a self-help Job Club where a small group of people meet every week or so to provide suggestions and encouragement to each other. Retraining should also be viewed as a support group. Yet, some unemployed people do not make the most of such opportunities.

What is your attitude toward searching out and taking full advantage of all the help available to you? If you are willing to accept other people and available agencies as "partners" in your search, give yourself a high score. If you prefer to go it alone, perhaps feeling you are "above" seeking help from others, give yourself a much lower score. Many people permit personal pride to keep them from accepting the kind of guidance and help they need.

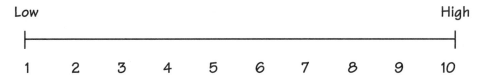

11 Creating Your Own Job

Sometimes, after exploring all available possibilities to get on a payroll with all the benefits, individuals decide to set up their own positions in their own homes. Some contract to do work (freelance artists); others build a clientele for special services (consultants); still others set up a small business (landscaping, auto repair, etc.) with only a minimum of overhead expenses. Many people are anxious and willing to take an off-beat, part-time job to hold them over financially until they can get a small operation of their own started. Have you fully investigated such possibilities? Do you have entrepreneurial instincts? Do you have a profession or special talent that lends itself to your operating as an individual?

If you think your resumé communicates the possibilities of independent work and *you are highly motivated in this direction,* demonstrate your interest by giving yourself a high score. If, however, you have no interest in this category, give yourself a score of 1.

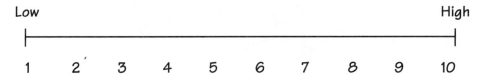

12 Goals: Self-Discipline

Goal-oriented people usually find it easier to win a new job than those who do not set goals. In fact, those who consistently set and reach personal goals are seldom out of work in the first place. Why? Because they usually have a Plan B ready to put into operation the moment their Plan A job loses luster or disappears. They do not wait until they are unemployed to test their marketability and they view networking as an insurance policy against unemployment.

Successful job-seekers should set goals for themselves at three levels. Level One: The number of interviews they seek each week. Level Two: The review and restructuring of techniques and strategies each month—often with the help of a professional. Level Three: Setting a time limit (three months?) to find and accept the best job available. Two other factors are involved. First, the individual is sufficiently flexible to adjust goals not achieved without undue frustration. Second, when a goal is achieved, the individual gives himself or herself a suitable reward.

Based upon your past experience and intimate knowledge of yourself, please rate yourself on the degree of self-discipline you possess in reaching realistic goals. Consider the rating system below as a *determination scale*.

Low   High

| 1 | 2 | 3 | 4 | 5 | 6 | 7 | 8 | 9 | 10 |

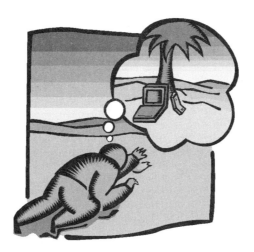

Constructing Your Profile

Please study the diagram below. Notice that each of the 12 categories are listed along the top. Also, notice the scale from 1 to 10 in the left hand margin. Your job is to return to your first rating (attitude) and place the number circled in the first column at the appropriate point on the scale. When you have transposed all 12 scores to the correct columns, connect the dots and you have your profile.

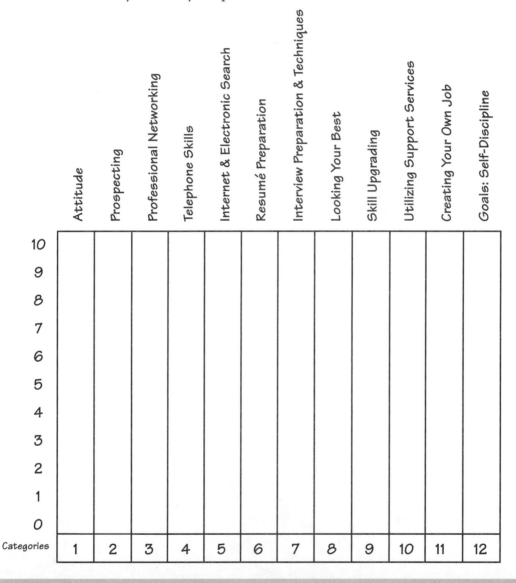

Please consider the above profile a preliminary step. After you have completed this book you will be invited to build a second profile to match with this one. This will enable you to measure the progress you have made or go directly to the chapter that addresses your weakest areas and start building those skills.

CHAPTER 1

Attitude

"I am convinced that life is 10% what happens to me and 90% of how I react to it."

Charles Swindol
From "Plain Talk," Wilmington, NC

What Is a Positive Attitude?

On the surface, attitude is the way you communicate your mood or disposition to others. When you are optimistic and anticipate successful encounters, you transmit a positive attitude and others respond favorably. When you are pessimistic and expect the worst, your attitude often is negative and people will tend to classify you as a person they would just as soon avoid. Inside your head, where it all starts, attitude is a mind set.

(It is the way you look at things mentally.)

REMEMBER:
YOU NEVER HAVE A
SECOND CHANCE TO MAKE
A FIRST IMPRESSION!

YOUR ATTITUDE TOWARD THE JOB-FINDING PROCESS

If you don't expect to find the best job available, you probably won't.

To earn a position equal to your potential, it is vital to maintain a positive attitude over an extended period of time. To measure your current attitude toward the job-finding process, complete this exercise. Circle the appropriate number between the opposite statements. For example, if you circle a 5, you are saying no improvement is possible.

	High				Low	
I like searching for prospective employers and setting up interviews.	5	4	3	2	1	I hate having to find a prospective employer.
I love the challenge of an employment interview.	5	4	3	2	1	Interviews bother me.
The prospect of a professional job search excites me.	5	4	3	2	1	I'm depressed before I get started.
An interview can be a dignified experience.	5	4	3	2	1	Interviewing is a demeaning experience.
Going through a dozen interviews to get the best possible job doesn't bother me.	5	4	3	2	1	I hope my first interview is my last.
Selling employers on my talents is fun.	5	4	3	2	1	Having to sell myself is embarrassing.
I want to learn everything I can about the job-finding process.	5	4	3	2	1	I'd rather have someone just offer me a job, or pay an agency.
Interview mistakes can be a positive learning experience.	5	4	3	2	1	Interview mistakes leave me totally discouraged.
Finding a job is a game: I'm going to win!	5	4	3	2	1	Finding a job is like going to the dentist.
I plan to complete three interviews next week.	5	4	3	2	1	I'm taking next week off; job-searching is tiring.

Total Score_____

If you rated yourself above 40, you have an excellent attitude toward the search ahead. If you rated yourself between 25 and 40, you appear to have some adjustments to make. A rating under 25 indicates you are not mentally prepared for your search. Please read on and take this survey again once you have completed this book.

 SELF-CONFIDENCE SCALE

You may have rated high in attitude, but if you do not have the confidence to meet those who interview you, all is lost. This exercise is designed to help you measure your self-confidence. Read the statements and then circle the number you feel best fits you.

	High				Low
I can convert new co-workers into friends quickly and easily.	5	4	3	2	1
I can attract and hold the attention of others even when I do not know them.	5	4	3	2	1
I enjoy new situations.	5	4	3	2	1
I'm intrigued with the psychology of meeting and building good relationships in a new work environment.	5	4	3	2	1
I know I am capable of doing a good job for a new employer.	5	4	3	2	1
When dressed for the occasion, I have confidence in myself.	5	4	3	2	1
I do not mind using the telephone to make appointments with strangers.	5	4	3	2	1
Large groups do not intimidate me.	5	4	3	2	1
I enjoy solving problems.	5	4	3	2	1
Most of the time, I feel secure.	5	4	3	2	1

Total Score_____

If you scored high on both the attitude and self-confidence exercises, you have a winning combination as far as winning a job is concerned. If you scored lower on self-confidence than attitude, you are receiving a signal that you need more experience dealing with people. This program can help increase your self-confidence.

MIND OPENER

But I'm Not a Self-Confident Person

David J. Schwartz, in *The Magic of Thinking Big,* presents one of the best explanations of low self-confidence ever found. He states that much lack of self-confidence can be traced directly to a mismanaged memory. He writes:

> Your brain is very much like a bank. Every day you make thought deposits in your "mind bank." These thought deposits grow and become your memory. When you settle down to think or when you face a problem, in effect you say to your memory bank, "What do I already know about this?"

Let's say you are getting ready to talk to people who are in the job or industry where you want to work. You sit down by the phone and you say to yourself, "I always have trouble doing this."

The "teller" in your memory bank will automatically supply you with proof that what you are thinking is true. "Remember last Wednesday when you called _____ and you could barely get the words out?" "Remember that crabby secretary who kept telling you how busy her boss was?"

Wait a minute. Don't touch that phone. There's a better way. Let's start over.

Let's say you are getting ready to do some informational interviewing. You sit down by the phone and this time, you say to yourself, "I need to know that I can do this. I need some kind thoughts, please."

Your "teller" supplies you with some different proof this time. "Remember how your friend, Sam, always tells you how friendly your voice is on the phone?" "Remember when you got put on hold for what seemed like ages, but you used the time to imagine yourself getting your job? And when the receptionist got back to you, she couldn't believe how energetic and positive you sounded?"

The kind of thoughts you ask for are the ones you'll get. The "teller" lets you withdraw the thought deposits you want to withdraw.

Schwartz then makes two suggestions that will build confidence and improve the management of your memory bank.

1 **Deposit only positive thoughts in your memory bank.** Do not dwell on negatives. Instead, when you're alone with your thoughts, recall things you've done that made you feel good. Just before you go to sleep, recall what you are thankful for: your spouse, children, friends, health. Think about positive or helpful things you saw people do today. Recall your accomplishments, even the little ones.

2 **Withdraw only positive thoughts from your memory bank.** If you never use your negative thoughts, they become weaker and lose their power to take away your self-confidence. When you do use negative thoughts, they become bigger than they were in the first place. So when you remember any situation, focus on the good parts of it and ignore the bad. This makes you feel better. This increases your self-confidence.

Food for Thought

> *"It is difficult to say what is impossible, for the dream of yesterday is the hope of today and the reality of tomorrow."*
>
> Robert H. Goddard
> American physicist and rocket expert
> 1882–1945

 # Self-Confidence

A *positive attitude* and *self-confidence* are partners when it comes to searching for and winning the best possible job. It takes self-confidence to arrange an interview and self-confidence to go through a successful interview.

You need not be a fast-talking extrovert to get a good job. Sensitive, quiet people often do better even when the qualifications are the same—providing their inner confidence and positive attitude shine through.

Sometimes it gives your self-confidence a boost when you list your good qualities. If you have trouble doing this, ask a friend to help you. Normally, you project greater confidence to those who know you better than you realize. Please list as many positive characteristics about yourself as you can in the spaces below.

1. _____

2. _____

3. _____

4. _____

5. _____

6. _____

7. _____

8. _____

9. _____

10. _____

11. _____

12. _____

The eight adjustment techniques in this section provide practical suggestions that can help you retain your positive attitude or, if necessary, restore it. It is recommended that you complete the exercises that go with each technique–*as you go!* In this way you can discover which techniques best fit your personal comfort zone.

ADJUSTMENT 1

Employ the Flipside Technique

The pivotal factor between being positive or negative is often a sense of humor. The more you learn to develop your sense of humor, the more positive you will become. The more positive you become, the better your sense of humor.

Some people successfully use the "flipside technique" to maintain and enhance their sense of humor. When a "negative" enters their lives, they immediately flip the problem over and look for whatever humor may exist on the other side. When this is successful, these clever folks are able to minimize the negative impact the problem has on their positive attitude.

Jim was devastated when he walked into his apartment. Everything was in shambles, and he quickly discovered some valuable possessions were missing. After assessing the situation, Jim called Mary and said: "I think I have figured out a way for us to take that vacation trip to Mexico. I've just been robbed, but my homeowners insurance is paid up. Why not come over and help me clean up while we plan a trip?"

When the garage service manager handed Megan her repair bill, she was shocked and could hardly hold back the tears. As she got out her checkbook, she heard another customer say: "Ouch! What a bill! I guess my car doesn't love me anymore. Oh well, no one said this love affair would be cheap." Megan introduced herself, and later, after they became friends, she learned that Richard had the wonderful habit of "flipping" bad news into something he could handle on a more humorous vein. It was a characteristic she learned to appreciate and imitate.

Humor in any form helps resist negative forces. It can restore your perspective and help you maintain a more balanced outlook on life.

How do you define a sense of humor?

A sense of humor is an attitudinal quality (mental focus) that encourages an individual to think about lighter aspects others may not see in the same situation.

Humor is an inside job. Humor is not something that is natural for one person and unnatural for another. One individual is not blessed with a pot full of humor waiting to be served while another is left empty. A sense of humor can be created. With practice anyone can do it.

Laughter is therapeutic. Just as negative emotions such as tension, anger and stress can produce ulcers, headaches, and high blood pressure, positive emotions such as laughter can relax nerves, improve digestion and help blood circulation. Dr. William F. Fry, Jr., a psychiatrist and associate clinical professor at Stanford University Medical School, maintains: "Laughter gets the endocrine system going." Of course, it is not appropriate to laugh away all serious problems; but anytime you can laugh your way into a more positive focus it will help you cope with your problem.

A "funny focus" can get you out of the problem and into a solution. Simply finding the humor in a situation won't solve a problem, but it can lead you in the right direction. Laughing can help transfer your focus from the problem to possible solutions. Using the flipside technique starts the process.

Why not give the flipside technique a try? You will discover that finding something humorous that you can share with others will cause your attitude to adjust faster.

To assist you to build this helpful habit, a special flipside exercise follows.

*Well, I said I needed
sunglasses and an umbrella—
Now I have both!*

 FLIPSIDE EXERCISE

Most problems have a flip or humorous side. Please list one or two negative situations to which you are currently adjusting in the left column below. Examples might be a job change, new boss, or a different work schedule. Or it might be a financial matter such as a surprisingly high bill or an expected rent increase. Once accomplished, use the right column to identify any humor you might generate on the flipside. Keep in mind that if the technique were easy to employ, more people would do it.

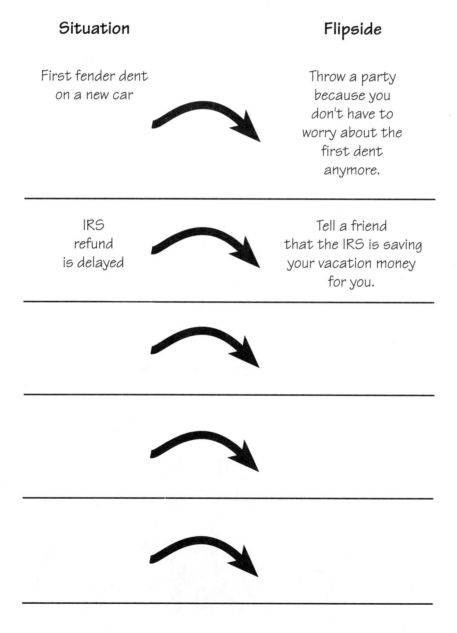

Situation | Flipside

First fender dent on a new car → Throw a party because you don't have to worry about the first dent anymore.

IRS refund is delayed → Tell a friend that the IRS is saving your vacation money for you.

ADJUSTMENT 2

Play Your Winners

When retailers discover a certain item is a "hot seller" they pour additional promotional money into the product. Their motto is: "Play the winners—don't go broke trying to promote the losers."

This same approach can help you adjust and maintain a positive attitude. You have special winners in your life. *The more you focus on them the better.*

Julie has what she calls "her special times." Examples are listening to classical music, taking walks on the beach, and enjoying good times over food with selected friends. Of course, Julie also has negative factors. Right now, she is bored with her job and is in the middle of a difficult conflict with an ex-boyfriend. She manages to remain positive, however, because she has learned to play her winners.

Jason, at this point, has more losers than winners in his life. He is trying to lose weight, is deeply in debt, and his car seems to live in the shop. Two positive factors in his life are his job (Jason is making progress in a career he loves) and running. By pouring his energies into his career plus running five miles each day, Jason has not only been able to maintain a positive attitude, but his weight is under control and he just got a raise. This happened because Jason knew how to play his winners.

All of us—at any stage in our lives—deal with both positive factors (winners) and negative factors (losers). If not alert, losers can push your winners to the background.

When this happens, it is possible to waste energy by dwelling on your misfortunes. Allowed to continue, your outlook will become increasingly negative, and your disposition will sour. Only you can change this. *Your challenge is to find ways to push the losers to the outer perimeter of your thinking.*

How can you *do this?* Here are three simple suggestions:

1 THINK *more about your winners.* The more you concentrate on the things you do well in life, the less time you will have to think about the negative. This means that because your negative factors receive less attention, it is not unusual for many to resolve themselves.

> Gerald frequently keeps a daily dairy about events in his life. He consciously stresses positives when making entries in his diary. As he falls asleep at night, he thinks about new entries he can make the next day. Gerald claims this technique helps him fall asleep faster and gives him a better start the next day.

2 TALK *about your winners.* As long as you don't overdo it (or repeat yourself to the same person), the more you verbalize the happy, exciting events in your life, the more important they will become for you. Those who drone on about the negatives of their situation do a disservice to their friends and, even worse, serve to perpetuate their own negative attitude. By playing their losers over and over, they wonder why they are not winning.

3 REWARD *yourself by enjoying your winners.* If you enjoy nature, drive somewhere and take a nature walk. If music is a positive influence, listen to your favorite song. If you enjoy sports, organize a game.

You play your winners every time you think or talk about them, but obviously the best thing is to enjoy them. If you are a golfer, playing 18 holes will do more for your attitude than simply thinking or talking about it.

Food for Thought

> *"There is only one success—to spend your life in your own way."*
>
> Christopher Morley
> American writer
> 1890–1957

PLAY YOUR WINNERS EXERCISE

List five positive factors in your life (include people, activities or anything else that keeps you positive). Where possible, use a single word.

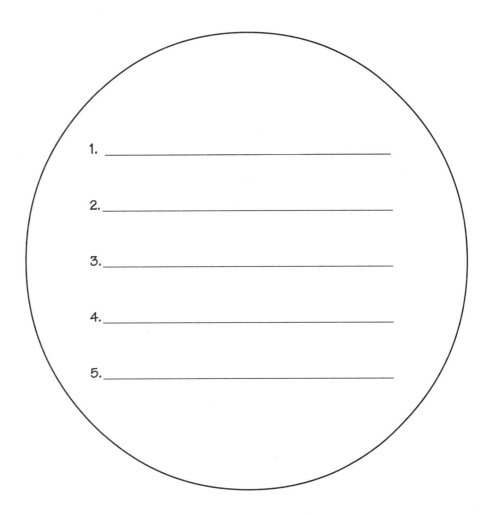

1. _____

2. _____

3. _____

4. _____

5. _____

You have just demonstrated there are powerful, beautiful, positive factors in your life. They constitute your winners. Play them!

ADJUSTMENT 3

Simplify! Simplify!

Some individuals unknowingly clutter their lives with negative factors, which makes it difficult for them to be positive. They surround themselves with unnecessary problem-producing possessions, people or commitments. Then they complain about the complexity of their lives.

The answer, of course, is to free yourself from complications. *Out of sight is out of mind.*

An uncluttered focus allows you to accept and enjoy life's simple pleasures. It is not distracted by a host of things that can drag you down.

To discover how you might make an adjustment to simplify your life, read the following five "clutter areas" and determine if any apply to you.

 CLUTTER AREA ASSESSMENT

Clutter Area #1: Unused and unappreciated possessions. Some people surround themselves with more tangible goods than they need or have time to enjoy.

Sometimes people own something they would be better off without. Getting rid of anything you don't need, use, appreciate or enjoy can simplify your life—and improve your attitude.

❏ Applies to me   ❏ Does not apply to me

Clutter Area #2: Too many involvements. Some people, in their desire to "do good" and gain acceptance, overextend themselves.

People who are generous with their time and talents sometimes don't realize that over commitments can cause them to become hassled. Consequently their efforts become counterproductive.

❏ Applies to me   ❏ Does not apply to me

Clutter Area #3: Career-home imbalance. Some individuals devote so much time and energy to their careers, they leave their home life in shambles. These workaholics forget that an unhappy home life can influence their attitude and cause them to turn negative in the workplace.

If people with both career and home commitments want a win-win situation, they need to do a good balancing act. This often means rearranging priorities so that both arenas are simplified.

❏ **Applies to me**   ❏ **Does not apply to me**

Clutter Area #4: Putting off the little things. Some people have the opportunity to "throw out" many negatives that enter their lives, but they procrastinate and keep these distractions around. Ultimately a buildup of minor negatives injures their outlook.

Each life contains some minor unpleasant tasks. If they are eliminated with dispatch, they will not take a severe toll on one's attitude.

❏ **Applies to me**   ❏ **Does not apply to me**

Clutter Area #5: Holding on to worn-out relationships. Some of us have a few "friends" who have become negative and need to be eliminated from our daily lives.

It is never easy, but in some situations it is necessary to terminate negative people-relationships to protect your attitude. This should be done quickly and without guilt. (It can be a more difficult matter when it comes to career or family relationships. In these cases, you must often be satisfied to simply insulate your attitude against such negative forces. See Adjustment 4.)

❏ **Applies to me**   ❏ **Does not apply to me**

The flipside technique (Adjustment 1) will help you see more humor in situations. Playing your winners (Adjustment 2) will enhance the impact of positive factors and reduce the impact of the negative. When you succeed in simplifying your life, you will find more beauty in it.

SIMPLIFICATION EXERCISE

Things I promise to do to simplify my life.

1. _____

2. _____

3. _____

4. _____

5. _____

6. _____

7. _____

8. _____

9. _____

10. _____

Food for Thought

> "Everything should be made as simple as possible, but not simpler."
>
> Albert Einstein
> American physicist, inventor
> 1879–1955

Adjustment 4

Insulate! Insulate!

It would be asking the impossible to think that all negative factors in our lives could be eliminated through any of the previous methods suggested in this book. Everyone, at some point, must learn to live with certain no-win situations that cannot be easily solved, thrown out, or ignored.

Almost everyone, including those with positive attitudes, has lived through a period working for a difficult boss. Others have managed to stay positive in spite of a family problem that defies solution. Still others have found a way to cope in a positive manner despite an illness or handicap that is permanent.

What is the answer?

Work to insulate your focus against the negative factor. Employ techniques that isolate or detach these negatives so they cannot impact too strongly on your attitude. Find methods to push them to the outer perimeter of your focus in order to reduce them in size and keep them at bay.

The following section reveals adjustments people often make to keep a major negative under control. Think of them as Phase I insulators.

Phase I Insulators

- Keep busy
- One day at a time philosophy
- Play your winners
- Exercise
- Use humor

- Simplify your life
- Concentrate on positive thoughts
- Do something for others
- Spend time with a friend

Long-term problems have a way of lying dormant for a while, then surfacing with a vengeance, causing the loss of a positive focus. Sometimes these problems will reach crisis proportions.

What adjustments can one make when serious problems "flare up?" Following are ways five different people learned to deal with such a situation. View these as Phase II insulators that allow you to keep the problem in perspective while you work on ways to solve it or learn to cope with it.

1 **Iris talks it out.** Whenever Iris faces a recurring problem, she makes her attitude adjustment primarily through intimate discussions with close friends. Like letting air out of a balloon, she reduces the problem to size by getting it out of her system.

"I learned long ago that every so often I need to verbalize my major problems to put them into perspective. It is sometimes hard on my friends, but I pay them back by listening when they need to talk."

2 **Jack works it out.** You can always tell when Jack is dealing with a big problem by he intensity of his activities.

"Work has always been therapeutic for me. When I am faced with a difficult situation that seems to defy solution, you'll find me cleaning out the garage, clearing brush or working overtime at the office. When I pour my energy into an unrelated job my problem seems to get smaller."

3 **Michelle laughs it out.** To deal with her no-win problems, Michelle refuses to take anything seriously. This approach—a kind of psychological immunity—seems to protect her positive attitude.

"I know it sounds crazy; but, when I can't deal in a normal way with one of my problems, I do bizarre things like roller skating to work, or wearing a funny hat until I have made my adjustment. I joke around until the problem becomes more manageable."

4 **Justin changes his environment.** When an "old problem" starts to nag Justin, he goes to the mountains where he claims a new perspective is possible.

"I'm a getaway person when the going gets rough. A change of scene pulls my focus back to the positive side. Don't ask me why."

When major problems start to upstage your positive attitude, Phase I techniques are helpful, but sometimes these more drastic adjustments (Phase II) are required.

Each individual should design her or his attitude adjustment program. What works for one person may not work for another. The following exercise may help.

INSULATION ASSESSMENT

The suggestions below may help you insulate your attitude against negative factors for which you do not have an acceptable solution. Read the complete list and place the number 1 in the box opposite the suggestion you like best, number 2 in the box of the idea you like second best, and continue until the list has been prioritized.

❏ Refuse to assume responsibility for other people's problems.

❏ Play your winners. Concentrate on factors that are positives for you.

❏ Find ways not to worry about things beyond your control.

❏ Talk problems over with good friends or professional counselors.

❏ Use the "flipside" technique; keep things light.

❏ Keep busy; work out problems through physical activity.

❏ Make a temporary change in your environment—take a long drive or a mini-vacation.

❏ Do something to help others.

❏ Engage in a special leisure activity (hobby, sports, card games, running, hiking, etc.).

❏ Other: _____

_____

ADJUSTMENT 5

Give Your Positive Attitude to Others

When you are frustrated by the behavior of others, you may be tempted to give them "a piece of your mind." This is understandable. It is a better policy, however, to give them "a piece of your positive attitude." When you do this, it allows you to readjust your attitude.

> Sharon asked Casey to meet her for lunch, because she needed a psychological lift. Casey didn't feel like it, but she accepted and made a special effort to be upbeat. When the luncheon was over, Casey had not only given Sharon a boost, she felt better herself. Both parties came out ahead.

When you give part of your positive attitude to others, you create a symbiotic relationship. The recipient feels better, but so do you. It is interesting but true that *you keep your positive attitude by giving it away.*

When it comes to giving your positive attitude to others, you can be generous and selfish at the same time.

> Mrs. Lindsey is considered a master teacher. The primary reason is that she freely shares her positive attitude with students and colleagues. In return, students and fellow teachers are constantly reinforcing Mrs. Lindsey's attitude with compliments and attention.

Everyone winds up a winner by sharing positive attitudes with others. The exercise that follows may help you decide which ways are best for you.

ATTITUDE GIVEAWAY EXERCISE

Below are different ways people share their positive attitudes. Some may appeal to you; others will not. Check *three* that fit your style—and that you intend to incorporate into your behavior.

- ❏ Going out of my way to visit friends who may be having trouble with *their* attitudes.

- ❏ Being more positive around those with whom I have daily contact.

- ❏ Transmitting my positive attitude to others whenever I use the telephone.

- ❏ Sharing my positive attitude by sending token items such as cards or flowers to those I care about.

- ❏ Sharing my sense of humor through more teasing, telling jokes, or using the "flipside" technique.

- ❏ Being more sensitive as a listener so others can regain their positive focus.

- ❏ Laughing more so my attitude will be infectious and others will pick it up.

- ❏ Communicating my attitude through upbeat conversations, paying compliments to others, etc.

- ❏ Giving my attitude to others by setting a better example as a positive person.

As you implement your choices, remind yourself that the more you give your attitude away, the more positive it will remain.

ADJUSTMENT 6

Look Better to Yourself

We are constantly bombarded through advertising to improve our image. Most messages claim that with a "new look" you will find acceptance and meet new friends.

"Discover the new you. Join our health club and expand your circle of friends."

"Let plastic surgery help you find a new partner."

Self-improvement of any kind should be applauded, but the overriding reason for a "new image" is not to look better for others; rather it should be because you want to look better to yourself. When you improve your appearance, you give your positive attitude a boost.

The term *inferiority complex* is not in popular use today; however, this old textbook definition is still valid: *An inferiority complex is when you look better to others than you do to yourself.* In other words, when you have a negative self-image, you make yourself psychologically inferior.

The truth is that you often look better to others than you do to yourself. There may be periods when you feel unfashionable, unattractive or poorly groomed. This does not necessarily mean you look that way to your friends, but you end up communicating a negative attitude because you don't look good to yourself.

When you have a poor self-image, it is like you are looking through a glass darkly. When you feel you don't look good, nothing else looks good to you.

When you look good to yourself, the world seems brighter. You are more in focus.

> When my wife, Martha, and I were first married, she had her hair done each Friday. It was a ritual. Sometimes, when our budget was tight, I wasn't sure it was necessary. What I didn't realize at the time was how much it helped her outlook. Granted, it improved her appearance; but that was not the important thing. What was important was that Martha looked better to herself. It took me awhile to realize that Friday was often our best day together.

IMAGE IMPROVEMENT EXERCISE

Below are five general physical and psychological activities people engage in to improve or maintain their self-images. Place a checkmark next to those that fit your personal comfort zone.

❏ **Wardrobe improvement.** Pay more attention (and money, if necessary) to what you wear, how you coordinate various fashion items, colors, etc. Make the best "fashion statement" possible.

❏ **Hairstyle, cosmetics.** Spend more time with your hairstyle, facial appearance, etc.

❏ **Looking healthy.** Devote time to an exercise program. Anything that will create a healthier appearance. Include posture, dental care, weight control, diet, etc.

❏ **Being yourself.** Refuse to be overinfluenced by others and the media. Stay with your own idea of what your image should be. Be different in the way you want to be different.

❏ **Image-attitude connection.** Accept the premise that your attitude will suffer if you don't keep a good self-image. Even if you don't care about how others think you look, care about how you look to yourself because it is important to your own attitude.

If one or more of the five remain—and you make progress in that area—you can expect to become a more positive person.

Food for Thought

"First say to yourself what you would be; and then do what you have to do."

Epictetus
Phrygian Stoic philosopher
c.A.D. 50-c.A.D. 138

ADJUSTMENT 7

Accept the Physical Connection

Apparently no one has been able to prove conclusively a clinical relationship between physical well-being and attitude. Most, however, including the most cynical of researchers in the area, concede there is a connection. Please answer the following questions and compare your answers with those of the author.

 PRETEST

True   False

❑   ❑   1. Exercise can do as much or more to adjust your attitude as a cocktail hour.

❑   ❑   2. Following a good diet has nothing to do with improving your self-image.

❑   ❑   3. The better you feel physically on a given day, the more positive your attitude is apt to be.

❑   ❑   4. Neither a sense of physical well-being nor a positive attitude can be stored indefinitely.

❑   ❑   5. Daily exercise can do little to keep one positive.

Author's Answers: 1. T (both will change your focus, but exercise is better for you and lasts longer); 2. F; 3. T; 4. T; 5. F (daily exercise is an outstanding attitude adjuster).

More than any previous time in our history, our nation is aware of physical fitness. A surprising number of us incorporate daily workouts into our schedules. This commitment to the "attitude connection" is expressed in this typical comment.

"My workout does as much for my mental state as it does for my body."

 BALANCING EXERCISE

In my desire to become a more positive person, I recognize that I may need a better balance between mental adjustments and physical exercise. To achieve this goal, I intend to do the following:

Daily Exercise Program	Weekly Exercise Program

ADJUSTMENT 8

Clarify Your Mission

It has been noted that an individual with a purpose is more apt to have a positive attitude than someone without direction. It need not be an all-consuming mission that reaches for the stars, but it should be sufficiently strong to provide a steady, ongoing challenge.

Mrs. Payne lost her husband in an automobile accident when their two sons were babies. Since the accident, her primary purpose in life has been to do the best job possible raising her boys. Mrs. Payne is so dedicated to her goal she refuses to allow herself negative attitudes.

Harvey discovered he had musical talent while in junior high school. Today, at age 40, he works as an engineer during the day and plays piano in a local restaurant at night. Harvey's dominant interest in life is his music. He is happiest when sharing his musical talents.

Emma spent years as an administrative clerk in a retail store. One day her boss asked her to fill in for a salesperson who phoned in ill at the last moment. Emma enjoyed the new challenge so much she redirected her life toward sales. Today she is a senior buyer at the largest store in town.

A mission in life provides direction, helps individuals achieve better focus, dissipates fears, provides perspective and destroys uncertainty.

Having direction gives a person a stronger grip on her or his attitude. The negative is easier to control.

Charlene has always liked nature. This interest has led her to a mission whereby she does everything possible to protect and preserve the beauty of her environment. As a second grade teacher, Charlene teaches her students to respect all living creatures. She shares with them the beauty in everything that grows. Her purpose takes her beyond the classroom. She is an active member of a leading environmental group and has had a number of nature articles published. Asked to state her activities in simple terms, Charlene said: "I want to leave my environment more beautiful than when I arrived."

It is difficult to picture Charlene without her mission. It provides her with recognition and identity, and a positive outlook on life.

Some people throw up their hands in despair when it comes to finding a primary purpose in life. They profess, "I don't want anything to control me. I don't need a special challenge. I just want to live day to day." Many of these people may wonder, at times, why they are not getting more out of life.

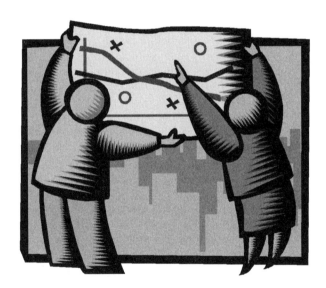

MISSION EXERCISE

Searching for or clarifying a life's purpose can be fun. To assist you in this process, you are invited to answer this question.

What would be your primary goal if you had one year to live and you were guaranteed success in whatever you attempted?

Answer the question by drawing or sketching a picture, design or symbol that represents your primary purpose. (Mrs. Payne would probably sketch two children; Harvey might draw some musical notes.)

Draw your design inside the circle without using a single word.

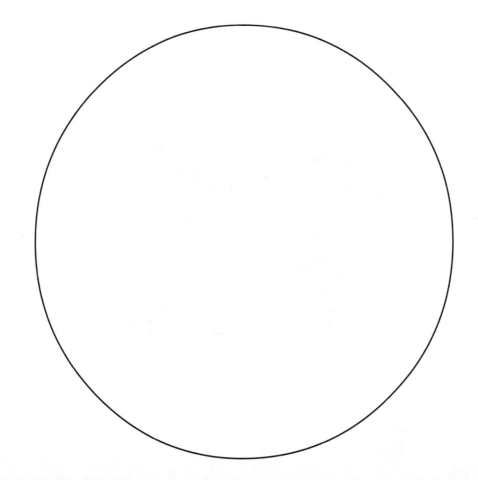

Whatever you draw could be your primary purpose in life. Think about ways you can help it become a reality. Good luck!

 REVIEW

Although all eight of the **Attitude Adjustment Techniques** can be used to both maintain and *restore* a positive attitude, some may be more effective for you than the others. If you feel one of the adjustment techniques is more effective in helping you *maintain* a positive attitude, place an X in the first column. If you feel a technique would be more effective in helping you *restore* a positive attitude, place an X in the second column. Should you feel a technique would be *equally* effective in both areas, place an X in both columns.

		Maintain	Restore
1.	Flipside Technique	❏	❏
2.	Play Your Winners	❏	❏
3.	Simplify! Simplify!	❏	❏
4.	Insulate! Insulate!	❏	❏
5.	Give Your Positive Attitude to Others	❏	❏
6.	Look Better to Yourself	❏	❏
7.	Accept the Physical Connection	❏	❏
8.	Clarify Your Mission	❏	❏

You may wish to remove this page and post it in an appropriate location where it will act as a reminder. It might help weave those techniques you want to employ into your behavioral patterns.

CHAPTER 2

Prospecting

"Prospecting: Search for, look for, seek, quest after or for, pursue, hunt (for), try to find, be after."

Reader's Digest
Oxford
Complete Wordfinder

It's the System You Use that Makes the Difference

Like a miner looking for gold, job-seekers must locate employers who need their services and are willing to pay competitive wages. You will probably find you spend more time "prospecting" than you do preparing for and completing job interviews.

As a job-hunter, just what is a prospect?

A prospect is an employer with the potential to make you happy as an employee. One with whom it is worth your time, energy, and commitment to make contact. Not all potential employers are qualified prospects. To be qualified means an employer should be prepared to: (1) make use of your skills (2) provide you with the salary and benefits you require and (3) make you an offer now or in the immediate future.

In periods of lower economic activity, some job-seekers may need to temporarily lower expectations.

When it comes to prospecting, most job-seekers make three fundamental mistakes. These are:

Mistake #1: Underestimate the time required and techniques that must be learned. As a result, many wind up accepting jobs beneath their potential. Finding the *right* interview situation is critical.

Mistake #2: Devote too little time to the search. It is easy to think that preparing for and keeping interviews might take a majority of the time involved to get the best job. Don't believe it! Sometimes the ratio of time spent to get a good interview is five to one. That is, it might take 10 hours to get a good interview possibility and only two hours to complete the interview (including transportation).

Mistake #3: Not following a prospecting system. To do a professional job of prospecting requires an organized, consistent approach. A helter-skelter attitude toward prospecting will not normally produce good results.

Traditional Resources

The first step in professional prospecting is to identify sources for prospective employers who have positions in concert with your life goal(s) and who will fit your needs as an applicant. Once a source has produced a qualified prospect, you should telephone to verify the information and begin planning to arrange for an interview appointment. Below are some of the resources available to most job-seekers.

 Prioritize the list by placing a check opposite the resource that you feel will produce the best prospects for you. Continue your ranking until you identify the one that will produce (in your opinion) the fewest or weakest prospects. Effective job-searchers use many resources.

❑ **Newspapers.** Classified and help-wanted ads, especially Sunday editions. (Some job-seekers attach appropriate ads to their resumé when seeking an interview appointment.)

❑ **Radio.** Many companies now advertise jobs on the radio and there are specialized talk shows related to careers.

❑ **Campus placement offices.*** Most colleges have placement services and you normally need not be a current student or graduate to participate.

❑ **Internships.** Sometimes volunteer agencies and some operating organizations offer temporary intern positions for students (and others). These can be from a few hours per week up to full time for limited periods of time. The intern has an excellent chance to learn more about a given organization or profession. The employer on the other hand has a chance to observe the intern with a possibility of offering a full-time position. Internships can also produce an excellent source for letters of recommendation.

❑ **Campus career centers.*** Here you should be able to do serious research on local employers, learn about Civil Service jobs, examination announcements, etc.

❑ **Temporary employment agencies.** Temporary agencies can provide extra income and potential leads during a job search. They expand opportunities to convert a temporary job into a permanent one. You have the added benefit of being able to look over a potential employer carefully.

*Note: A telephone call to a local university or community college will verify if services marked with an * are available.*

❑ **Networking.** This means making personal contact with mentors (caring advisors such as teachers, former employers, family members or friends). Anyone who may be able to lead you to a worthwhile interview should be reached through networking (which is discussed in detail in the next section).

❑ **Interviewing for information.** Friends, relatives or co-workers will probably be able to refer you to qualified people who may be willing to discuss the "pros and cons" of the kind of work you are interested in. These "insiders" can often provide prospecting and interviewing tips and sometimes prospecting referrals.

❑ **Private employment agencies.** Normally a fee is involved—but some can be helpful. Check these out carefully before making any commitments.

❑ **Trade magazines and associations dealing with your career area.** Many have Help Wanted ads and job banks.

❑ **State Human Resource Offices.** In addition to providing prospects and job finding seminars, these offices often handle unemployment insurance activities.

❑ **Job Fairs.** A company can sponsor a job fair to help recruit for one or several types of openings. Many times job fairs are sponsored by a third party like a college. These job fairs have representatives from many different companies trying to recruit for the same type of job or a variety of jobs.

❑ **Job Club.** A Job Club is when people with comparable qualifications group together to help each other. You might be smart to spearhead the formation of such a club. Some communities, often under the sponsorship of the State Human Resource Department, organize Job Clubs.

❑ **Annual reports.** In these reports, organizations describe their plans for future expansion, new products and services, or shifts in emphasis from past practices. These can be signals to prospect for jobs that will soon be open. These reports may be obtained from firms by writing to the Public Relations Director at their headquarters, or from your local library.

❑ **Public Library.** Your public library has a wide variety of resources. Ask the reference librarian to help you.

❑ **Internet.** Company information such as annual reports, product information and job postings can be found on a company's web site. In addition, you can post your resumé for employers to find.

❑ **Others** (List Your Own):

_____

_____

LIVE PROSPECTS EXERCISE

(WORTH AN INTERVIEW)

An organized prospecting system (featuring networking) should provide a job-seeker with a *continuous* list of promising interviews. For a person job hunting on a full-time basis, the system (fully operational) should normally produce two or three legitimate prospects per week. Remember, a legitimate prospect is one worthy of an interview and interviews require time, transportation and energy.

To get started, you may wish to list a few prospects in the spaces below *now*. You will be adding new prospects on a continuous basis. Securing a promising interview is not a signal to stop prospecting. If the interview does not produce a job you have wasted valuable time.

Prospective Employer	Name of Contact	Telephone

CHAPTER 3

Professional Networking

"Network: A group of people who exchange information, contacts, and experience for professional or social purposes."

Webster's Collegiate Dictionaruy

An Emphasis on Networking

As you position yourself for a new career opportunity, you may decide to draw upon a wide repertoire of job search methods. You can especially benefit from varied approaches if you are clearly well-qualified for the work you seek with a direct track record of applicable job experience.

Obvious channels of information about jobs include advertisements, agencies, or search firms, and personnel offices. They are not hard to find and focus on filling budgeted openings. Perhaps you know people who have found jobs this way. Maybe you have landed a job yourself using these resources.

If a traditional method of job search works for you, great! If you become aware of a special position that seems made to order, go for it! Opportunity may come from many different sources, all valid and worthwhile to explore, all potentially productive.

However, experts say that about 80 percent of jobs are found through the hidden job market, the informal channels of communication between employers and job-seekers. What conclusions might you draw about preferred job search strategy?

The Case for Networking

If you place a premium on matching yourself with compatible roles and settings ...

If you value keeping the initiative as you conduct your search for work ...

If you want to access more job opportunity than standard sources publicize ...

If you would like to position yourself favorably with people with power to hire ...

Networking will be for you!

Networking, in plain and simple terms, means reaching out to other people for advice, information, feedback, and referrals. It is an information exploration of possible opportunities. It builds bridges to find out about needs you can meet, and is a mechanism for talking with people you would probably never know about or get through to if you were to use more formal job search methods.

Networking gives you tremendous freedom to target where you would really like to work, meet outside of competitive selection processes, find out about real and compelling hiring needs. You gain the interest of key people who can hire you, open doors for you, or leverage you to be hired by friends and colleagues.

Through traditional job search means, you find out about a limited slice of opportunity. This is heavily tended by gatekeepers whose primary function is to screen out anyone but the most obviously, formidably, well-qualified candidates.

Through networking, you find out about posted openings and get a helping hand in competing for them AND you find out about employment options that are not yet published, budget requisitions in the pipeline for authorization, operating needs in departments that will shortly be the source of staffing requests, and problems you could address as a temporary consultant. To use your resumé for optimal results, consider the benefits of networking as you plan your own job search strategy.

PERSONAL NETWORKING EXERCISE
(ONE CONTACT LEADS TO ANOTHER)

Please use this page to list those special individuals who are *already* part of your networking system. To be on your list you should feel comfortable calling them to guide you to prospective employers. Once these people are listed (*please* include telephone numbers) you are ready to add new members to your network. Do not add a name until you have built a potentially mutually rewarding relationship.

> *Please keep in mind that anyone on this list can lead you to another, who may in turn lead you to another, who will offer you the job you seek.*

Name	Phone Number
_____	_____
_____	_____
_____	_____
_____	_____
_____	_____
_____	_____
_____	_____
_____	_____
_____	_____

A systematic way to implement this program would be to start a 3x5 card index file with contact names and telephone numbers, along with other information such as comments about who referred you and the field they represent.

Use these contacts and conduct some informational interviewing.

Informational Interviewing

What is informational interviewing?

It's quite easy. It's simply talking to people about the jobs you're interested in. It's a way to learn what skills, attitudes, and results employers look for in their employees. It is *not* a job interview. It may lead to one, or even result in a job offer, but that is not its main purpose. Your main goal is to do research; to get the information that will make your job search easier and shorter.

How do you proceed?

Clearly state to an employer or worker that you only want some information. Tell this person you are not asking for a job. All you want is to know more about the business and its needs.

People love to talk about their work

If you ask the right questions and really listen to the answers, you'll learn much that will help get you back to work—in the job you want.

Who do you talk to?

Talk to the person who sets the standards for the position you want. This is the person who makes the hiring decisions. This may be the foreman, office manager, owner, or someone else. It almost always is *not* someone in the human resource department.

Should you interview in person or on the phone?

Most employers don't mind taking a phone call and may give you 10 to 15 minutes to answer your questions. In fact, most seem to prefer phone calls.

Using the phone is also quicker and cheaper for you. You can contact more employers over a wider geographic area in less time.

If you would rather talk face-to-face, call first and set up an appointment. Walking in unannounced in the middle of a busy day is not usually a good idea.

What do you say?

An opening statement might go like this:

You: Hi, my name is _____. I'm considering a career change. I'm interested in learning more about the position of _____. I would like to talk with the person in your company who knows the most about kinds of experience, personal qualities, and skills needed to be successful as a _____. (Say this next sentence without pausing.) I am looking for some information to help me make my career decision.

The person that you initially speak to will most likely be a secretary/receptionist or some other nondecision maker. There are several responses he or she might make at this point.

Receptionist: We don't have any jobs available.

You: That's OK. I'm not looking for a job today. I am simply looking for some information. I have just a couple of quick questions to ask so I can make some good career decisions.

Receptionist: The person you need to speak to is not in right now. Can I take your name and have them call you back? (This is almost always a dead end.)

You: I'm away from my phone a lot and I would really hate to miss the call. It's really no problem for me to call back at a more convenient time. Who should I ask for and when do you expect them in? *(Write this information down; you can use it to call back later and ask for the decision maker by name.)*

Receptionist: Hold on, I'll put you through to _____.

You: Thanks. *(Congratulations. You just passed the first barrier.)*

You have the decision maker on the phone. Now, what do you say?

You: *(Identify yourself. Use that opening statement again.)* I'm not looking for a job today. I am simply looking for some information. I have just a couple of quick questions to ask so I can make some good career decisions. Do you have a minute?

Decision Maker: I don't have time for this.

You: When may I call you?

Decision Maker: We don't have any jobs available.

You: *(Repeat opening statement. I'm really not looking for a job today.)*

You can practice this with a friend or relative. Go ahead and ask some of your questions. Once you are comfortable, you can talk to real live employers.

When you are asking your questions, remember:

- People love to talk about their jobs.

- Take a real interest in what they are saying.

- Listen carefully. Restate briefly what the speaker has just said. Show him or her that you understood.

- Get the full name of the person you talked to. Be sure to thank that person for spending time with you.

You'll get valuable practice in:

- Contacting employers
- Listening to answers
- Asking questions
- Talking about your skills

Skills Statement – Opening the Door

Employers are busy people. When you call, they may be in the middle of serving a customer, repairing a machine, writing a report, fighting a headache, or meeting with an employee. When they pick up the phone, you can bet they are really still thinking about something else.

In the first seconds of your telephone call you must do two things:

- Get the employer's attention

- Interest him or her in talking further to you

> *A good skills statement does both.*

Your skills statement and telephone manner must quickly shift the employer from thinking about what he or she was doing to thinking about how talking to you can be of benefit.

A skills statement is three sentences long. It:

1 Identifies you by name to an employer.

2 States briefly the skills you have and the results you have produced in past jobs—skills or results that would be important to this employer.

3 Shows attitudes you have now or ways that you have fit into other work settings that would be important to the employer you are speaking to.

Saying these three sentences should take you one minute or less. You are not trying to convince employers to hire on the spot. You are not telling your complete employment history. You simply want to get attention and interest.

If you succeed, they may ask you to talk more or to answer some questions. This means that it is very important to have in front of you examples or names of references that can back up the statements you make.

Skills Statement – Example

If you have previous experience in the job: Your previous experience will help.

Barbara, who has one year of experience as a receptionist/clerical worker, might say the following:

First sentence:

Hello, my name is Barbara Wilson.

Explanation:

Identifies her to the employers.

Second Sentence:

I have one year of experience as a receptionist/clerical worker. I can file, type 45 wpm, operate a multiline phone system. Also, I am trained in several word processing programs.

Explanation:

States present skills or past results produced. Think back on the important parts of your past job. What did you spend most of your time doing? Did you find a way to do it better, faster, or more accurately? What skills did you need? What training did you receive?

Third Sentence:

I really enjoy working with the public. I can handle stressful situations and was employee of the month two times with my last employer.

Explanation:

Shows attitudes or how you have fit into other companies. What personal qualities or abilities did you need to do your job well? Are you good with the public, efficient, honest, loyal? Did you receive any awards? Were you dependable and on time?

Just for fun, time yourself saying Barbara's skills statement. It probably takes less than 30 seconds. Yet look at how much good information is in it.

Creating Your Own Skills Statement

It is time for you to create and write down your skills statements.

Remember these points:

- It should take less than one minute to say.

- It must get an employer's attention.

- It should make an employer interested in talking further with you if there is any need for your skills.

- It will work best if said in a friendly and energetic way.

Sentence 1:   Identify yourself.

Sentence 2:   State briefly the skills you have or results you produced on past jobs that are important to the employers you are calling.

Sentence 3:   Show how you have fit into other companies in the past or the personal qualities you have that are important to the job you are seeking.

 ## Your Skills Statement

Identify Yourself: _____

_____

Your Skills/Results: _____

_____

_____

_____

Personal Qualities: _____

_____

_____

CHAPTER 4

Telephone Skills

"We must accept finite disappointment, but we must never lose infinite hope."

Martin Luther King, Jr.
American clergyman and civil rights leader
1929–1968

Using the Telephone

Making employment interview appointments by phone saves time, transportation costs, and is professionally accepted. This exercise will help prepare you to do this more effectively. With your completed Prospect List in front of you, take the following steps:

Step 1: Dial number.

Step 2: While waiting for an answer put a smile in your voice. *(Actually smile so your voice will have a friendly tone.)*

Step 3: If you do not have a personal contact, when someone answers, ask to speak with the human resource office *(for a large company)* or the employer *(in a small company)*. Say: *"I'm looking for some information and would appreciate your help. I'm interested in learning more about the position of _____. I would like to talk with the person in your company who could answer a few questions."*

Step 4: When the party answers, give your full name and give your prepared statement.

Step 5: Communicate an upbeat, positive attitude. Whatever arrangements may or may not be made, be sure to thank the individual *by name* for the help you have received.

Step 6: Ask your contact for advice about any other steps you could/should take.

Step 7: Record date, time and location of any appointments. Be sure you have the name of the person you spoke to and clear directions on how to find the interview site.

 ## TELEPHONE EXERCISE

Place a check in the square if you agree with the following suggestions.

❏ Try to cluster your calls.

❏ Group your appointments. If you make a morning appointment some distance from your home, try for an afternoon appointment near your first interview.

❏ Always ask for directions and draw a map before you leave home.

Get Yourself Going

Do whatever it takes to start calling. And then, once you start, keep going. After the first call, write down the results and move on to the next. Make your 16 to 24 calls, congratulate yourself, and stop.

You may be wondering how many employers you will need to contact during the days or weeks you are using this method. The answer: as many as it takes. Keep contacting employers on a regular basis until you receive and accept a job offer.

The more employers you contact each day and each week, the quicker you will uncover openings, interviews, and offers. Other workers have found that 50 to 75 calls usually lead to a job offer.

Look at the Numbers

If you use one morning each week for calling, you will probably contact 16 to 24 employers per week.

If you use two mornings, such as Tuesday and Thursday, for phone days, you may reach 32 to 48 employers per week.

If you use three mornings, such as Monday, Wednesday, and Friday, for contact days, you can reach 48 to 72 employers per week. Remember: that's our average number of success. Could it happen to you? Do you suppose you might be considering a job offer in only one week?

There's another good reason for making all these calls. Repeating this process will make you feel comfortable with it. What's more, you will also get better at it. Sure, you may be nervous at first: dry lips, shaking knees, those butterflies in your stomach, headache, nausea, and so on.

However, I guarantee that you will find after 10 (or 20 or 30 or 40) calls that you are more relaxed and natural with the people you speak to. You will even find that you have some enjoyable conversations. You may even begin to look forward to making calls. That's what practice can do for you.

The more employers you make good contacts with, the sooner you will uncover openings, interviews, and offers. There is just no substitute for these contacts.

Where to Find Businesses and Phone Numbers

1 **The Yellow Pages.** These frequently list the name of the owner, manager or the decision maker.

2 **Friends, relatives, family members, past employees.** It is truly amazing how many people you will find who know just the right person for you to call.

3 **Chamber of Commerce.** A stop here may provide you with directories and listings of businesses as well as lots of names of contact people.

4 **Libraries.** These are a "must stop" for the prepared job-seeker. Here you will find many directories. Ask the librarian how to locate and use:

- Your state's *Directory of Manufacturers*

- Contacts Influential

- Trade journals

- Magazines

- *Thomas' Register*

- *Standard and Poor's Register of Corporations, Directories, and Executives*

5 **Back issues of newspapers.** Look at the want ads from one or two years ago. Since one to two years is a typical turnover rate, you may find a number of these positions open again. Make a list of the employers who advertised jobs that you want. Call these companies and speak with the decision makers.

6 **Most companies have Web sites where you can find information.** Also, many of the publications you would find at the library are now accessible from a computer. This includes newspapers and yellow pages!

> **The more employer contacts you make, the more interviews you will have, and the sooner you will find the job you want.**

Telephone Tip Sheet

Keep this tip sheet handy when you are ready to make your telephone calls to employers. Review it briefly before you start and have it in front of you each time you call.

Before you call:

1. Set up a schedule of when you will make the calls. Have clear goals. *For example: "Today I will call 24 employers."*

2. Make your initial calls in the morning. Return calls in the afternoon.

3. Plan and practice what you will say. Call your friends, family, relatives, or any helpful person and practice on them.

4. Practice your skills statement.

5. Write down potential questions and practice answering them.

When you call:

1. Have your skills statement, resumé, and application fact sheet in front of you.

2. Smile when you're talking on the phone. That smile will come through to the person on the other end of the line.

3. Be enthusiastic. Vary the level of your voice. Avoid a monotone.

4. Make a mental picture of the person on the other end of the line. Talk *with* them, not at them.

5. Ask for a face-to-face meeting.

Getting past the secretary:

1. Ask for the decision maker by name.

2. Sound confident, as if you should be speaking to the decision maker. *Because you should be!*

3. Ask for the decision maker's direct dial number.

And remember:

1. Set goals.

2. Be persistent.

3. Ask for a face-to-face meeting.

CHAPTER 5

Internet & Electronic Search

"As a general rule, the most succesful man in life is the man who has the best information."

Benjamin Disraeli
English statesman and author
1804-1881

1 Plan

Researching on-line has two benefits. First, by using the Internet, you gain hands-on familiarity with a tool that is taking the business world by storm. Challenge yourself to try out the search engines, push the limits in searching for information on topics and visit the sites.

So much information is available from the resources on the Internet that you could easily become overwhelmed and lose your motivation. Focus your job search on the Internet with the following steps:

- Pay a "virtual visit" to companies that interest you and bookmark their sites so that you can return there easily.

- Identify industry-related Web sites using the same search techniques.

- Search for listservs that represent people in the profession or industry you want to explore or in which you wish to network.

Food for Thought

> "Destiny is no matter of chance. It is a matter of choice: It is not a thing to be waited for, it is a thing to be achieved."
>
> William Jennings Bryan
> American lawyer and politician
> 1860–1925

Staying Focused

The Internet can be fascinating. Surfing—or simply following links from site to site—can consume a lot of time. You will need to sort out the enormous amount of information you can access. You will find distractions of all kinds and could spend an entire day (or night) on-line, with nothing to show for it. These distractions can get out of control, diverting you from searching for a job. The following tips will help you stay focused.

- **Set up a to-do list for your sessions.** This will help you stay on track, getting the information you need and producing results for your search.

- **Decide in advance what information you are looking for.** Resist the temptation to follow links from the original site. Instead, give yourself a specific amount of time to visit the site or follow links, and then come back to your research.

- **Allot some casual surfing time.** You know what other obligations you have. Decide how long you can spend playing. Even during this time, it's wise to keep your goals in front of you so that what you do still applies to your search.

- **Unsubscribe from lists that don't produce for you.** Downloading and reading 50 nonrelevant e-mail messages is not the best use of your time. If you need to stay subscribed to stay up-to-date, make a file and spend a specific amount of time doing the reading.

- **Set up a file system of mailboxes for your e-mail messages.** Download your e-mail, answer and file it. Group all the e-mails on a specific topic or from a certain person, and then transfer them to your file mailboxes all at once, deleting those of no interest.

- **Set up your browser to bring up the home page of the newspaper** whose classifieds you find most useful or of your professional association. Simple to do, this will keep your target in front of you.

- **Stay out of chat rooms** and avoid doing other nonessential on-line activities, or use those activities as rewards for getting specific tasks done and out of the way.

- **Be aware of your "body clock"**—if your energy is low in the evening, get up an hour earlier and use your best creative time to do the tasks.

- **Have a plan.** Job searching is work: know what you want to accomplish, do that and get off-line.

Action Item

Visit the site at http://www.paradesa.com and check out the Digging for Data section of Learn the Net.

2 *Get Organized*

Sticky notes on the light switch and phone numbers and URLs (uniform resource locator—the addresses of Internet sites) jotted down on the back of your birthday card won't help you feel productive. At the very least, you will need to learn to set up file folders (for storing mail) within your e-mail program, bookmark sites you want to visit frequently, and a use a three-ring binder with tabs to organize research about companies and contacts.

Since your odyssey may take you to distant companies and evolve over the next months or years, start as you want to continue. Build habits that will make it easy for you to spend time on essential career management functions instead of devoting half a day to searching for contact information that you put on the back of a take-out menu.

Create Your Own Cyber-address Book

Use material in this section to:

- Create and organize your electronic job search addresses

- Record addresses that you get when you aren't near your computer

- Track contact dates and keep your list current

- Prepare data for entry into your computer-based system

- Minimize lost information and searching for the best contact you've made

Log Your Contacts

Photocopy of the next page onto three-hole-punched paper. Put these pages behind alphabetized tabs.

Consider color-coding the pages by whatever logic seems appropriate to you—for example, using blue paper for places where you can post your resumé, green for addresses of local associations, and so on.

Use a standard three-ring binder or your personal organizer binder, whichever will make it easier for you to use the information.

Contacts

Name:
Title:
Address:
Phone: Fax:
E-Mail:
URL:
Contact Dates/Referral Source:

Name:
Title:
Address:
Phone: Fax:
E-Mail:
URL:
Contact Dates/Referral Source:

Name:
Title:
Address:
Phone: Fax:
E-Mail:
URL:
Contact Dates/Referral Source:

Name:
Title:
Address:
Phone: Fax:
E-Mail:
URL:
Contact Dates/Referral Source:

Better yet, take another step into the future! Why use a low-tech way to keep track of high-tech resources? You will want to spend more time collecting resources than organizing them on paper. Figuring out which site is which often requires more searching than it's worth. As sites move and new URLs replace old ones, an electronic address book format may be a simpler way to keep track of these resources.

Some of the best solutions may already be on your computer. New technology in datebooks, laptop calendar planners, or palmtop machines allows you to download information onto your computer. Use these features to become a premier networker. Staying in touch with prospective employers doesn't happen by accident.

Create a URL log

Bookmarking the Web sites you visit as you explore the Internet is the most efficient way to work. That way you will be able to go back again and again very quickly. However, your collection of URLs will probably grow from other sources as well (for example, networking contacts, newspaper or magazine articles or ads, or even informal discussions on noncareer-related subjects). So much information is available that it's critical to stay organized. Creating a URL log is also a good idea, so that you can keep track of the resources available at various URLs, even when you're away from your computer. Following is a sample and some suggested uses for such a log:

- Copy the next page onto heavy card stock and include it in the various sections of your job search binder to organize specific information for each industry.

- Laminate a copy of the next page and use it with an erasable marker to note possibilities as you read newspaper or magazine articles.

- Take a copy to a networking meeting or professional association and ask each person you meet to add a URL.

URL Log

URL	For

3 Ask for Help, Input and "Air Time" with Others

On-line career centers are not just for resumé/job posting. Visit their career coaching and information sections, post to mail lists and ask questions. You have the ability to network globally. Take advantage of it. Staying connected keeps you going if the job search gets tough.

Internetworking should support—not supplant—your person-to-person networking activities. A key advantage of using the Internet for networking is that it allows you to be active even when you have only a few minutes to spare or if you can't get to a specific meeting because of travel or timing.

Tips for Successful Internetworking

- Visit sites that list associations, discussion or interest groups or user groups that might know about jobs in your field or industry.

- Subscribe to listservs and read them for a few weeks. Post to them when you have something of interest to say or a question you would like discussed.

- Collect e-mail addresses of people you connect with at "live" functions.

- Surf the Web and e-mail comments or questions to the Web master at sites that catch your interest.

- Visit Web sites of companies in your industry. Read about how they prefer to receive resumés, what jobs they have open and how they identify themselves in the market.

- Develop a few personal commercials that have been spell-checked, edited and can be cut-and-pasted into your messages as needed. These should be snippets of information about you that are clear, concise, and easy to include when developing written replies.

- Neatness counts! On-line postings show your writing skills. Spelling errors, typos, and grammatical slips are not allowed. If your resumé says you have excellent written communication skills, it should show in your on-line posting.

- Become a "switchboard," passing along information about jobs or industry issues to others.

- Give information…do not expect that you will only be the recipient. Contribute to on-line forums.

- Pay attention all the time. A strong network can be important for doing your job, or advancing your career.

- Create a personal business card that you can give out.

- Create a matching on-line business card "signature" for your e-mail.

EXERCISE: BRAINSTORM THE POSSIBILITIES

Jot down names or immediate possibilities for a start at Internetworking.

Internet Tool	Activity	Names, Possibilities
e-mail	• Stay in contact with former associates, friends, and family at very low cost. • Write to trade journals and professional associations for lists of employers. • Send resumé to newspaper ads that list e-mail addresses. • Request information about products and projects from Web sites.	
listserv	• Subscribe to and read mail lists of interest (from industry or functional perspective) for one week. • Contribute ideas or answer questions. • Ask for information about places to post resumés or make contacts.	
Usenet newsgroups	• Search newsgroups for discussion groups of interest. • Post articles or comments • Ask for information.	

Job Search Vocabulary

Speaking the language of your industry or job function is very important; however, as you start your cybersearch, you will learn a whole new vocabulary based on the terms you will see used on-line. Some key Internet terms are listed below along with some on-line job search buzzwords and acronyms you will find in the ads. At http://www.paradesa.com you'll find a complete Internet glossary that is updated regularly. Print yourself a copy.

ASCII text: Basic text files that allow only the use of standard keyboard characters in upper and lower case. Most e-mail programs use ASCII as a standard, because it can be used by any type of computer. ASCII text resumés are an important part of any on-line job search.

Applicant Tracking Systems: Computer-based systems that organizations use to compile information about applicants. These systems scan, read, organize, store, and retrieve resumés on demand. They may also allow candidates to confirm that their resumé or application has been entered into the database and may generate a response to applicants to confirm receipt.

BBS (bulletin board system): A system that lets users connect to a specific computer where they may exchange information, files, and discussion comments.

Database: A structured archive of related information, such as a computerized file of job postings that can be searched or a compilation of resumés stored for employers to search.

Freenet: A bulletin board system that provides free community information such as current events and school calendars. Many offer free access to the Internet, including e-mail capability.

Key Words: Specific industry, job component, skill or functional terms by which an employer may search a database. Example key words are database management, teamwork, materials control, cash flow analysis, creative design, and continuous process improvement.

Key Word Resumé: A resumé that includes a category specifically for key words, making it easier for a computer search to read the information and find matching qualifications.

Kiosk: Commonly used for retail directories or interactive information presentation, employment kiosks present job-seekers with information or on-screen applications to complete.

On-line Help Wanted Ads: Classified employment ads that can be accessed by computer at any time. Examples are on-line ads at the *San Jose Mercury News, The Wall Street Journal,* or *Today's Careers* Web site at http://www.todays-careers.com. In addition, some services provide job-seekers with subscriptions to job ads in specific occupations in any area of the country. For example, E-Span (http://espan.com) will mail you eight matching job descriptions every week once you register.

Resumé Database Service: Firms that register candidates in their databases and permit employers to draw from their databases when recruiting to fill openings. Fees for service vary; listings may target specific geographic regions, industries or skills.

Reading the Postings

Common abbreviations you should know about when reading on-line postings.

AA/EOE	=	Affirmative Action/Equal Opportunity Employer
BA	=	Bachelor of Arts
BS	=	Bachelor of Science
BSBA	=	Bachelor of Science in Business Administration
CNE	=	Certified Network Engineer
JD	=	Doctor of Law
DOD	=	Department of Defense
DOE	=	Department of Energy
MBA	=	Master of Business Administration
MS	=	Master of Science
M/F/D/V	=	Male/female/disabled/veteran

List others that you find in the job postings you read:

_____

_____

_____

_____

CHAPTER 6

Resumé Preparation

"Know Thyself ..."

Socrates
Greek philosopher of Athens, generally regarded as one of the wisest people of all time
469 – 399 B.C.E.

A Positioning Step

Having your resumé at hand is an important positioning step for attaining new employment. With it, you know you can quickly respond to an attractive job opportunity. Your resumé gives employers a clear message that you are interested in being considered for a position.

Your resumé is a factual document about your history. It symbolizes your interest in new horizons. Your decision to write your resumé is a commitment to your career management. It shows you are becoming change-ready in a very practical and important way.

A Job Search Ritual

A resumé is a ceremonial job search practice, widely expected and used. It is a traditional tool in hiring and job seeking, and plays a key role in communications between employers and applicants.

A resumé may be a powerful conveyor of meaning, or serve as a routine formality. By developing a resumé, you make a vital and valuable statement about yourself, and gain a very effective resource.

Contrary to popular belief, resumés do not have to be written only one way. As long as you are honest about yourself, you have tremendous freedom to be creative.

Resumé Myth-Busting

You may have some unlearning to do as you think about your new resumé. A whole series of limiting notions has grown up around resumés. If you find yourself believing that a resumé should be written only one way, think again.

Your resumé is not a job application form, with a standardized set of information. It is a highly individualized statement of your work interests and related assets. Let go of attachments you have to ideas about content and format, categories and sequence, and see what emerges. Consider the following:

- An effective resumé is a sales tool, not an autobiography.

- A descriptive resumé is easy to write; a persuasive resumé is what works.

- Draw material for your resumé from any area of your life.

- Emphasize experiences that best support your objective.

- Influence the way others see you by the way you see and describe yourself.

An Exercise in Personal Growth

When you move beyond a basic summary of background information probing into what makes you special, writing your resumé can be a very powerful exercise in personal growth.

A Source of Insight

Defining the focus of your resumé requires careful thought. Consider what you would really like to do, what you think you can do, and how much you want to do it. Your focus will include issues of:

Meaning: How satisfying is the work that you have been doing? Does it make sense to maintain your current career focus?

Purpose: What do you want to do in your next job? What kind of career involvement draws you and excites you?

Risk-taking: How big a change would you like to make, if any? How comfortable do you feel in following your heart?

A Source of Self-Esteem

Get set for a thoroughly enjoyable side-effect of resumé writing. Identifying your personal qualities and attitudes that support your effectiveness is highly pleasurable and a tremendous source of self-esteem. While it may take some effort to focus in on your most important assets, you are likely to enjoy what you discover and feel very proud of yourself.

Thinking about what you do best, defining the ways in which you make a difference, in which you have an impact, recalling examples of excellent performance, of personal contribution…this is a good prescription for rainy days, not just resumé development!

Describing your strengths helps you build and strengthen a positive self-concept. This serves as a reminder of your capabilities and potential during hard times in your career. And it helps you to feel and project confidence when an employer asks the predictable questions: "Why are you here?" "What can you do for me?" and "Why should I hire you?"

Persuasive Case-Building

What information would an employer most appreciate knowing about you, and what would establish your ability as a contributor? What attitudes do you have that suit you to the work you would like to do? Which of your life experiences are most relevant to describe? What skills and accomplishments would be most useful to highlight?

A Job Search Paradox:

All *of your experience counts;* some *of your experience applies.*

When you write your resumé, you look at the full range of your life experience as potential source material. In assessing items for inclusion, there are no artificial distinctions made between paid and unpaid experiences, recent and more distant experiences. Experience is experience.

Your greatest achievement may have been the volunteer work you did for the United Way. An extracurricular school activity may be the basis of many important activities which recommend you for employment. A project on your job which falls outside your regular responsibilities may be the most striking indicator of your interests and abilities. A special accomplishment in an earlier job may date back in time, but be well worth citing.

At the same time, the principle of selectivity applies. Why is a particular personal quality or experience important to cite on your resumé? How does it strengthen your candidacy? Is it a miscellaneous detail taking up space, or is it a vital part of persuasive case-building?

Producing Your Resumé

Producing a resumé takes commitment. It means devoting the time to each step to achieve a strong end result. You can quickly generate a resumé if circumstances require, but you need to deal with each step even as you expedite completion. There are no shortcuts in the process, only intensification of effort. Quality comes from attention to every detail, from start to finish.

You may find it useful to review The Eight-Step Formula before beginning work on your own resumé. Getting the "big picture" of the production process will give you a sense of the purpose of each of the steps and how they all fit together. Noting issues and techniques of special relevance to your situation will make it easier to think strategically about the handling of your own experience.

Your resumé is a highly personal and important document. It should clearly support your objective, reflect what makes you special in language you are comfortable using, and have graphics that are thoroughly professional. Resumé production makes the most of what you have to offer for the work you want to do.

The Eight-Step Formula

Step 1: Define Your Objective

Step 2: Assess Your Marketability

Step 3: Select Your Format

Step 4: Build Your Base

Step 5: Develop Your Draft

Step 6: Refine the Quality

Step 7: Package with Care

Step 8: Run a Quality Check

1 Define Your Objective

Defining your objective is at the heart of developing a resumé. By zeroing in on what you want, you can feature the most *relevant* aspects of who you are and what you have done. You are creating a guide that will help you decide what to say about yourself, which will build your case for work opportunities you are best suited to, and most desirable.

On Staying "Open"

You may say, "Ah, but what if defining an objective on my resumé eliminates me from being considered for a job I might not have thought of, but am qualified to do?" or "I want to keep my options *open*–open to anything that can be a source of income and stability, a toehold in an organization of interest."

Reciting your personal background for employers to evaluate will not catch the attention of an employer with very specific hiring needs. An unfocused resumé reduces your chances for becoming a successful applicant. Defining your objective will help you be noticed.

The Distinction of Personal Focus

On the average, resumés get a 30-second review. If your objective, what your contributing role can be, what area of the organization you are oriented to are unclear, you will probably never talk with a person with the power to hire or recommend your hiring.

Your challenge is to stand out immediately and impressively as an attractive candidate for employment. A focused, targeted resumé can make a highly positive first impression of you as a career-minded person, clear about your professional interests and persuasive about your related strengths.

An Inner-Directed Approach to Your Job Search

This approach means laying aside impulsive responses to job possibilities "out there," especially when there are a variety of unlikely openings listed in the weekly classifieds. It requires that you develop an inner compass to the kinds of work most likely to give you satisfaction and success, with faith in your inherent marketability while you pursue what you do best and most enjoy.

 A QUICK QUIZ

1. How clear is your focus on your professional identity?

_____

_____

_____

_____

_____

2. What kind of work do you want to be doing in your next job?

_____

_____

_____

_____

_____

3. Briefly describe your job objective.

_____

_____

_____

_____

_____

A Resumé Objective—Some Definitions

- A statement that specifies your preferred kind of work.

- A description of the contributing role you wish to play, or the function you seek involvement with, in your next job.

- Your short-term employment focus, supported by personal interests and skills.

- A realistic aspiration, emerging from your demonstrable experience base.

Note: Your objective is distinct from your ideal job, visions, dreams, and fantasies of career satisfaction—which may guide your thinking about occupational direction—but not be sources of your personal livelihood.

Achievable and Motivating

Notice the basic practicality of a resumé objective. It should stand up well under scrutiny and probing. You should be able to accomplish it.

If you are entering a line of work that your education directly qualifies you for or seeking a new opportunity based on your prior job experiences, defining your resumé objective will be fairly straightforward.

On the other hand, if you are seeking work with meaning for the first time or are changing careers into distinctly new and different work, then defining your resumé objective in even generically descriptive terms may be a challenge.

Food for Thought

> "We live in the present, we dream of the future, but we learn eternal truth from the past."
>
> Madame Chiang Kai-shek
> Chinese Socialist
> 1898

2 Assess Your Marketability

Your next step in developing a resumé is to carefully assess your marketability. Your task is to examine thoroughly the major pluses and minuses of your candidacy for the work you want. This process will help you identify your special selling points and assist you in handling areas of complexity.

Your Marketability

Assuming your job objective is based upon a significant interest and strength, and there is a need or demand for what you want to do, *you are marketable.*

You are a valuable potential employment resource in the world of work, defined as the exchange of skilled service for money and other benefits. For work in your target area, chosen after considerable reflection on its suitability for you, you have much to give. Your personal qualities make you an asset. Your experiences demonstrate your effectiveness.

Your task in marketing yourself is to communicate, with exquisite clarity the particular ways you can excel and contribute, with employers who have a need that you can meet. Your mandate—and your opportunity—is to build a compelling case for being hired, to demonstrate vividly why it is in an employer's enlightened self-interest to bring you on board.

Some Myths About Marketability

Some might have you believe that to be marketable you must be perfect. They claim you must match all specifications for a position, that no departure from an idealized profile will be tolerated, that you must conform in all respects to conventional definitions of "qualified."

Similar beliefs are that you should be neither too young nor too old, neither overqualified nor underqualified, and have no deficits in formal education, no gaps in your employment history, and no irregularities in who you are, what you look like, and what you have done with your life.

Furthermore, the party line of doomsdayers and naysayers holds that in difficult economic times it is too competitive to try anything you have not done before. They are convinced that going after work that you would enjoy is not practical or feasible and is a waste of time.

Finally, your gloomy advisors may sign off with admonitions about the importance of presenting yourself to employers in proper, standard ways—particularly on your resumé. They may advise you to use an extremely familiar format, outlining the chronology of your background. They may be sure that this will enable employers to best exercise their expert judgment on your appropriateness for a job.

Taking Control

If you have found yourself buying into such beliefs, it is time to take back control.

Your ability to influence employers' perceptions of you will begin with your perceptions of your own value and your firm commitment to demonstrate that value creatively and convincingly. You may need to push the limits of your own assumptions about qualifications, in thinking about which of your assets recommend you for employment.

 ## MARKETABILITY CONCERNS EXERCISE

Review the list and mark those that concern you.

❏ I am too young to be competitive.

❏ I am too old to be competitive.

❏ I do not have a college degree.

❏ I have too many degrees.

❏ My major does not relate to what want to do.

❏ I have no specialized training.

❏ I have no paid experience.

❏ I have no professional-level experience.

❏ My work experience is in a different field.

❏ I have been out of the job market too long.

❏ I have stayed on one job too long.

❏ I have not gotten promotions.

❏ I have changed jobs too often.

❏ I have gaps in my work history.

❏ I have been laid off.

List your other concerns:

_____

_____

_____

_____

_____

Marketability Concerns as Strategic Challenges

As you review your concerns about your marketability, keep this crucial point in mind: no aspect of your history or circumstances has the power to block you from your goals. This is a key operating assumption for writing a resumé *and* for managing your career!

In other words, you are in the driver's seat of how you look at your situation and influence others to look at it. When you really set your mind to it, you can determine, to an extraordinarily large degree, how you are perceived and evaluated.

It is practically a given that somewhere, somehow, something will pose a problem in job search communications. While complicating factors are likely to come up, how you deal with them is very much a matter of choice.

You may have one or more areas of potential complexity to address. You may need to give special attention and careful handling to how you present some fact or facts about yourself. You may have work to do on reassessing your beliefs and habitual ways of looking at matters that set you apart from a classically qualified candidate.

The idea is to remain in charge of your self-presentation, to be matter-of-fact in handling objections, and resourceful and positive in refocusing attention on your skills and related accomplishments.

Your confidence and strength in the job market will be directly proportionate to your ability to take your marketability concerns and treat them as strategic challenges.

Examples:

- If you are concerned about your age, you can de-emphasize or delete dates and bring out the strengths of your substantial experience.

- If you do not have a college degree, you can emphasize the strength of your job experience and employer-sponsored training.

- If your work experience is in a different field, you can focus on the transferability of your skills and any avocational bridges to your new line of work.

3 Select Your Format

Selecting your resumé format is a major strategic decision. Real and compelling differences characterize the two most common formats, which have impact on the receptivity employers have to your initiatives.

No universally "right" format is appropriate for all people. Your review of your own objective and background will be your most effective guide to selecting the best format for you.

The Chronological Format

Your employment record is the primary organizing principle for this format, a job-by-job historical narrative of your work effectiveness.

Kam Lee
500 Broad Avenue
Fortune, Ohio 44150
(216) 555-4772

Objective
Seeking to secure a position as a customer service representative with a company that will allow me to grow professionally and help the company achieve its goals.

Summary of Skills
- File maintenance
- Proficient in 10-key by touch
- Proficient in Microsoft Office Suite
- Telemarketing/customer survey completion
- Loan verification
- Able to work in a multitask, fast-paced setting
- Able to deliver quality customer service
- Detail-oriented, hard-working, and flexible

Employment History
Ran Temp, Inc.   Cleveland, OH
SYSCO Foods, Inc.
Data Entry Clerk   1999
- Assisted new hires on a 12-line phone system
- Located and corrected invoices to ensure correct payment
- Provided telephone customer service to input orders accurately and quickly

Kelly Services
Key Corp   Cleveland, OH
Office Support   1998 – 1999
- Conducted customer service phone surveys to assess quality of state contractors' work for final payment
- Verified loan information accurately and quickly
- Contacted customers for levels of satisfaction for results in improving quality of service

J.C. Penney Co.   North Randall, OH
Customer Service   1996 – 1998
- Processed incoming customer orders, using suggestive selling techniques to increase sales
- Provided merchandise to customers; resolved problems with incorrect orders quickly and efficiently

Education and Training
Cuyahoga Community College – Metro   Cleveland, OH
Call Center/Customer Service   2000
Certificate

Merits:

- This format accentuates your formal qualifications for the work you are seeking. Appropriate for directly qualified candidates with linear progression paths, it showcases the track record of clearly pertinent, often increasingly responsible, experiences. Seasoned judgment in grappling with job challenges is emphasized.

- Recruiters and some hiring managers are accustomed to, and often prefer, a traditional format. Many find it familiar, straightforward, and easy to use when making preliminary decisions of inclusion and exclusion.

Drawbacks:

- For candidates who are starting or changing a career, this format emphasizes the lack of direct, in-depth experience in the targeted career area. It under- scores past identity rather than future potential.

- Gaps in employment conspicuously brief or long affiliations and time periods elapsed since certain qualifying experiences are spotlighted.

- Rather than accenting accomplishments on and off the job, it lends itself to a somewhat dry, repetitive recitation of job responsibilities.

Criteria for Use:

- The chronological format is particularly effective for people with clear-cut qualifications, who are continuing or advancing in a particular career direction. It is acceptable for other less overtly qualified people. This format can be productive, if you cite relevant skills and tasks that support your objective within the job-by-job description.

Food for Thought

> *"The safest words are always those which bring us most directly to facts."*
>
> Charles H. Parkhurst
> American clergyman and reformer
> 1842–1933

The Functional Format

Your key skills, knowledge, and related accomplishments are the primary organizing principles of this format, citing relevant examples of effectiveness as proof and prediction of your ability to contribute.

Canterbury Services Inc.
Susan J. Sanders
500 Center Road #3
Warrensville, Ohio 44150
(216) 555-4637

- Technical writing
- Document formatting
- Press releases

- Copy editing
- Simple drawings for manuals
- Sales literature

Software

Word Processors: WordPerfect, Word for Windows

Desktop Publishing: Framemaker, Ventura Publisher, Pagemaker (Windows and MacIntosh)

Drawing Packages: CorelDraw, Visio

Other: Microsoft PowerPoint, Microsoft Excel

Experience

Fifteen years, primarily writing operating instructions for industrial control equipment. The equipment includes PLC interface software, PID loop software, combustion controllers, web guiding systems, and IEEE-488 bus interfaces. The writing includes hardware and software documentation, hard copy manuals, online help, and HTMLHelp.

Wrote published press releases, sales literature, and trade journal articles. Also prepared content for corporate Web pages.

In addition to practical writing experience, taught technical writing at Cuyahoga Community College, where I created my own class lectures, syllabus, and assignments. Also have experience teaching adult basic education courses (third grade and above reading levels). My B.A. is in English.

Information Gathering

Use information from project designer(s), product drawings, and, if possible, actual use of the equipment.

Output

PostScript or PDF. I also work with a firm that produces high-speed laser output of documents.

Merits:

- This format provides an opportunity to establish the transferability of skills and accomplishments for candidates who are starting or changing a career. Grouping these items in self-contained categories builds a case for your ability to function in a new situation. The conventional resumé format dilutes or contradicts this talent.

- Not limited to paid employment, you can give status to qualifying experience from every area of life. This format widens the scope of informal experience supportive of your career objective, including special projects, internships, community service, and relevant leisure pursuits. It eliminates distinctions that discount their importance.

Drawbacks:

- For directly qualified candidates with a linear progression path, this format challenges the standard presentation of personal strengths. Executive recruiters and other employment professionals prefer a job-by-job description to trace with clarity exactly what has been done, for whom, where, and when.

- Some employers assume that this format hides background information of importance.

- In a purely functional resumé, key time/space anchors that employers expect are not given. This information can be essential to credibility.

Criteria for Use:

- The functional format is particularly effective and highly recommended for people without direct experience in the area of their career objective. Since it accents skills and achievements, it is effective and often desired by people who are well established in a career.

Food for Thought

"Suit the action to the word, the word to the action."

William Shakespeare
English dramatist and poet
1564–1616

The Combination Format

The combination format recognizes the inherent drawbacks of both the chronological and functional formats used in their pure forms.

- The pure chronological resumé may be too mundane. It is descriptive, but tends not to be persuasive about personal qualifications.

- The pure functional resumé may be too free-floating and read like a set of assertions about abilities, unlinked to verifiable sources of confirmation.

- Whether you prefer the chronological or functional format, the most effective resumé blends the best elements of each.

Sarah Pike
20 Main Street
Pleasantville, Ohio 44111
(440) 555-7788

Career Objective
To obtain a professional position that will enable me to utilize my experience and education to benefit my employer while allowing for growth and increased responsibility.

Highlights of Qualifications
Banking and Customer Service
- Prepared customers' Owners/Lenders policies, averaging 30+ daily, increasing productivity by 150%
- Prepared and processed wire transfers and to verify balances
- Maintained cumulative balance of checks going through encoding machine while exceeding hourly keystroke requirements

Administrative
- Supervised and trained new and temporary employees
- Planned and implemented special projects
- Managed monthly budget of $50,000

Community Shelter Work
- Greeted families and provided intake services
- Made troubled families feel safe and secure
- Assisted clients with referrals for housing

Work/Volunteer Experience
- 1993 to Present: Administrative Assistant/Shelter Worker   Family Centers   Cleveland, OH
- 1997 to 1998: Customer Service Representative   First National Bank Cleveland, OH
- 1997: Encoding Specialist   Second Federal Bank Cleveland, OH

Education and Training
- 1999: Cuyahoga Community College   Earned certificate in Call Center/Customer Service
- 1992 to 1994: Cuyahoga Community College Major Course of Study: Business
                                            Admin./Word Processing

Skills
Knowledge: Microsoft Word, Excel, Word Perfect 5.0 and 5.1, Database Systems, Microsoft Works for Windows

---

The Chronological-Combination Resumé

This format retains the structure of a job-by-job delineation of experience and emphasizes accomplishments, the hallmark of the functional resumé.

The Functional-Combination Resumé

This format retains the structure of key skills, knowledge, and accomplishments; incorporating a distilled EXPERIENCE section, which denotes career-related time/space anchors, the hallmark of the chronological resumé.

4 Build Your Base

Develop a thorough database of your potentially qualifying experiences. This ensures that you consider all possible factors that support your career objective. Care with this step gives you a rich foundation to draw on as you write your draft. This enables you to write a quality resumé as quickly as possible. For greater flexibility, use separate sheets of paper to make your lists.

Review Your Learning Experiences

List the particulars of each academic program in your educational background:

- High school diploma, name of school, location, year of completion

- Name and location of each college or university attended, number of credits earned, focus of studies, degree, year of completion

- Merit scholarships, coursework relevant to your objective, research studies, theses, projects, internships, student leadership activities

List all career-related seminars you have taken, including noncredit workshops both in the community and on the job:

- Professional development seminars, sponsor and depth/duration

- Certificate programs

Review Your Work Experiences

Trace your employment record and other qualifying experiences such as community service:

- Title, organization, location, dates

- Responsibilities

- Accomplishments

Review Your Leisure Experiences

List your leisure pursuits, both present and past:

- Avocations

- Applicable skills and knowledge

- Accomplishments

5 Develop Your Draft

As you begin to develop your draft, remember that it is your first effort. It does not need to be marvelous. The challenge in the drafting phase is to generate thinking and phrasing that can be improved as needed.

Writer's block generally reflects an intimidating concern with perfection that makes it nearly impossible to write. Treat your draft as a preliminary exercise, an experiment in wordsmithing, and see what you get.

When you give yourself permission to take this approach to your draft, you will find that while the process takes thought and concentration, it is surprisingly manageable. The pressure for premature results is off.

Reserve a block of time that will be sufficient to write a good first draft—preferably a full morning, afternoon or evening. Remove distractions and interruptions. Get as comfortable as you can. Have your reference materials handy.

Reflect on what you want to bring out about yourself, jotting notes as you go. Take a deep breath and, step-by-step, write your draft.

Aim to write one or two pages. The length will depend upon your personal preference and the scope and depth of your experience that supports your objective. Be relevant, clear, and specific.

Core Elements to Develop

- Your contact information

- Statement of your career objective

- Summary of your qualifications

- List of your key skills

- Profile of your related experience

- Profile of your related education

- Citation of your related memberships

6 Refine the Quality

At this point, your task is to refine what you have written. Closely scrutinize your draft for every enhancement. Bring a gently critical perspective to examine it from every angle. Use a red pen or pencil to flag items you want to improve, change the emphasis, or delete.

Picture yourself as the hiring manager for a job you want. Does the substance of the resumé catch your attention? Are you impressed by what you read? Does it match a profile of the kind of person you could use on your staff? Does it create interest in getting together for an exploratory meeting? Would you schedule an interview on the basis of this resumé?

Now, picture yourself as an editor. Are you satisfied that there are no errors on the resumé? Does it hang together tightly? Does it seem organized in the most effective way? Is it easy and inviting to read? Would you sign off on this resumé as a top-notch example of effective writing?

 EDITING CHECKLIST

Selectivity:

- ❏ Do the items on your resumé support your objective?
- ❏ Have you de-emphasized experiences that are not clearly qualifying?
- ❏ Have you eliminated personal information like marital status and age?
- ❏ Does the language you use enhance your marketability?

Sequencing:

- ❏ Are your strongest categories presented first?
- ❏ Are the strongest items within your categories presented first?
- ❏ Do your headings and subheadings bring out your key selling points?

Tone:

- ❏ Is your language upbeat?
- ❏ Do you begin your sentences with strong action verbs?
- ❏ Have you avoided using personal pronouns?

Specificity:

❏ Do you focus on facts, offering concrete "for instances" of your strengths?

❏ Do you use written numeric figures to quantify your achievements?

❏ Do you use other objective measures when figures are not applicable?

Clarity:

❏ Are your thoughts well-organized, in clear sentences and paragraphs?

❏ Have you avoided jargon?

❏ Have you avoided abbreviations?

Simplicity:

❏ Do you use short words, sentences and paragraphs?

❏ Have you cut out redundancies?

❏ Can you condense, consolidate or delete anything for greater impact?

Consistency:

❏ Is your capitalization consistent?

❏ Are your verb tenses consistent?

❏ Do items of a similar nature have parallel structures?

Accuracy:

❏ Have you eliminated typographical errors?

❏ Is your spelling correct?

❏ Is your punctuation correct?

❏ Is your grammar correct?

7 Package with Care

A resumé that looks sharp gets attention and stimulates interest in its substance. When the content is in top-notch shape, your final task is to package it. Match the verbal standard you have set for yourself with an equally high visual standard. Let graphics help sell you.

Picture yourself in a first class advertising agency, charged with packaging your resumé in a tasteful, effective form. No frills, no gimmicks, just a quietly distinctive statement reflecting classic design principles. What criteria would you bring to set up the text? What would you watch out for and be careful not to do? How would you develop camera-ready master copy?

Now picture yourself as the production manager of the creative department. What printing process would you use? What paper would you select? What quality control measures would you take to ensure that every copy of the resumé is crisp and clear?

 ## PACKAGING CHECKLIST

Overall Impact:

❑ Does your resumé make a positive impression at first glance?

❑ Do the graphics enhance the communication of the information?

❑ Is it easy to find your crucial selling points?

Page Layout:

❑ Have you selected the standard 8 1/2" x 11" size for your page?

❑ Have you determined the relative merits of major formats for your needs—of left margin headings, centered headings or left margin headings with text underneath?

❑ Have you been consistent in your placement of headings and subheadings?

❑ Have you avoided justifying the right margin so that words are evenly spaced?

❑ Have you eliminated single words at the end of paragraphs and page starts?

❑ Have you used vertical spacing consistently, establishing well-defined groupings of information?

Highlighting:

❑ Have you made selective use of various techniques of emphasis, such as bolding, capitalization, bullets, underlining, punctuation, headings, and subheadings?

❏ Have you bolded and capitalized your name and major category headings?

❏ Have you used upper- and lowercase lettering in text entries, for readability?

❏ Have you made liberal use of bullets as the primary method of accenting brief, important entries like key skills and accomplishments?

❏ Have you used colons, dashes, and slashes to your advantage?

❏ Have you used headings to guide the reader through the major components of your qualifications, sequenced in order of importance?

❏ Have you used subheadings to spotlight groupings of qualifications of special importance, distinct from those of relative unimportance?

Typography:

❏ Have you focused on a time-tested classic typeface—a sans serif like Helvetica or a serif like Times Roman?

❏ Have you limited yourself to a maximum of two typefaces to avoid clutter and competition for attention with the message of your text?

❏ Have you sized your typeface for text between 9 and 14 points?

❏ Have you used a laser or ink jet printer, if printing the resumé yourself?

❏ Have you written explicit, detailed design specifications if you're using typesetting services?

❏ Have you proofread your master copy with rigorous care to ensure it is precisely as you wish, with no typos, misspellings, or other problems?

Paper:

❏ Have you selected a high-quality bond paper, with a high cotton fiber content?

❏ Have you chosen white, ivory, beige, or light grey for your paper color?

Printing:

❏ Have you selected a printing process for quality reproduction—using either an offset duplicator or an offset press?

Note: If you are planning to e-mail your resumé or you know the employer may be scanning your resumé, please review the Creating Your On-Line Resumé later in this section.

8 Run a Quality Check

Above and beyond your own careful editorial and packaging review, you may want to introduce one final quality assurance measure. It is often useful to evaluate your resumé through the eyes of one or more of your valued colleagues.

Consider contacts whose professional judgment you regard highly. Request a candid assessment of your resumé. Explain that you have given considerable time and thought to developing a strong statement about yourself to support your new career horizons, and you are substantially satisfied with its overall design.

Explain that you want to be sure that you have not overlooked anything that could affect its positive impact in your job search. You would appreciate any input that could enhance what you have produced.

Feedback from someone who is experienced in the career area you are pursuing is particularly valuable. You can count on solid understanding of the nature of the work, knowledge of important skills, and insight on the kind of experiences that may be most useful to emphasize.

A Caution

In a room of ten people, you will be apt to find ten different opinions about what makes a good resumé. There are a wide variety of perspectives on this subject. Many people subscribe to very conventional ways of presenting written qualifications. It may not be in your best interest to incorporate every suggestion.

The key point is to value your own judgment in filtering the ideas you receive. Make only those alterations that truly improve how you present yourself.

Field testing your resumé is good, solid marketing practice. It has the potential to provide excellent advice for fine-tuning your resumé.

Build in what you think is best. Then use your resumé with confidence.

A Dynamic Document

Resumé writing is an ongoing process. You may craft a splendid sales tool that represents you well in the job market at a certain time for a certain type of work. You may find that it is a very productive resource for achieving important short-term career goals.

Still, there is a built-in obsolescence to the information. It is a snapshot of your excellence up through *today*. By the very nature of what a resumé is designed to do—help you to acquire a new job opportunity—it loses value as soon as it proves its value.

As your experience base broadens, you will need to revisit what is important to say about yourself on your resumé. As your career goals evolve, you will need to take a fresh look at how to build the most convincing case for your candidacy for different or more senior work opportunities. As you progress, you will have new achievements to cite. As you develop additional qualifications, you will want to showcase them to your full advantage.

A Continuing Design Process

At its best, your resumé will change focus and form to reflect your emerging interests and strengths. The design that works for you at the entry point in your career may be limited in its ability to help you to advance. You may decide to treat certain experiences in a substantially different way, as time passes and you acquire more directly relevant qualifications. Or you may decide to make a career change in a dramatically new direction.

Using your resumé for optimal results means revising it as often and as extensively as your situation warrants. It means looking at your resumé as an evolving reflection of your career, redesigned as needed to feature the best of your ongoing growth and development.

Value-Adding Cover Letters

For optimal results, your resumé should be accompanied by a cover letter. Like your resumé, cover letters can be written on a very routine level or with high positive impact. At a minimum, a letter serves as a conveyance of your resumé. At its best, a letter adds value, communicates information over and above your resumé, which assists in positioning you for opportunity.

Personalized Communications

In sharp contrast to boilerplate generalities, a value-adding cover letter is a personalized communication. It emerges out of a very careful consideration of what you want to say to a particular person, who is a potential resource in your job search.

A value-adding letter *always* begins with the name of the intended recipient; it is always addressed to a specific person you have identified as beneficial to contact. It recognizes that hiring is a very personal process enhanced by personal contact at every step of the way.

Tailored Communications

A value-adding letter recognizes that individual recipients have individualized concerns. It shows an understanding of a particular context, a special set of conditions, a major emphasis of work. It makes explicit links between what you have done and what you would like to do, describing especially relevant experiences in more detail than the resumé alone can usually accommodate.

The cover letter is a valuable opportunity to bring out your enthusiasm for the work you seek, so show an understanding of an employer's priorities and concerns, and to spotlight certain personal qualities and background elements that make you notably well-qualified.

Persuasive Communications

The basic purpose of the letter is to stimulate interest and involvement. You want to motivate someone to consider hiring you or opening doors to others with hiring needs. You want to convince someone to meet you, advise you, introduce you, recommend you, sponsor you, etc.

So, consider carefully what you want to say and how you want to say it. Think hard about what information you can provide, what points you can emphasize, what language you can select to create allies and advocates for your initiatives.

STRUCTURING YOUR COVER LETTER MESSAGE

In your introduction

- Make a connection with your reader.

  Mention a prior contact or referral; reference an article written or a talk given; identify your response to an ad, etc.

- Define your purpose in writing.

  State your interest in an exploratory meeting or in following up on a preliminary contact; state your availability for an advertised position, etc.

In the body of your letter

- Provide a concise statement of the experience base you want to leverage.

  Number of years of experience in all aspects of…; a recent degree in…; extensive avocational pursuit of…; services contributed in…, etc.

- Express your enthusiasm.

  Use phrases such as "highly committed to…"; "a real passion for…"; "lifelong interest in…"; "what I most enjoy…"; "very appealing to…"; "very motivating and rewarding to…" "feel aligned with…" etc.

- Provide details specific to recipient's needs and interests.

  Highlight selected accomplishments; key themes in your prior work, applicable to your new focus; experiences from any area of your life that qualify and motivate you.

- Refer to your resumé.

  Use an introductory phrase such as: For your review, I am enclosing a copy of my resumé…; a profile of the "big picture" of my background…; a detailed review.

In your conclusion

- State your appreciation.

  Express, for example: Many thanks for…; your availability to meet…; your advice and perspective on…; consideration of my candidacy…; your thoughtfulness in.

- Establish the next step.

  State your interest clearly: I look forward to an opportunity to talk with you in the near future. I will call you in a few days to see if we could arrange a time to meet… I welcome the opportunity for a personal interview to discuss the strengths of my background and the range of contributing roles I could play.

A Sample of a Value-Added Cover Letter

Alex Coughlin
52 Orchard Ridge Road
Bridgeport, CT 06601
(203) 576-0138

Mr. Maurice Wilson, Sales Manager
Premium Soccer Lines, Ltd.
6642 Lincoln Boulevard
New York, NY 10010

July 14, 2xxx

Dear Mr. Wilson,

I am writing to you on the referral of Peter Strauss. In a recent conversation, he suggested it could be valuable to meet with you for your advice on developing a career in sales of soccer products, and to explore the possibility of a contributing role at Premium Soccer Lines.

I appreciate that you may not have an opening currently, nor know of one elsewhere. I would, however, find it valuable to talk with you for whatever perspective you may be able to give me on developing employment in this line of work.

Soccer is a real passion for me, and I am extremely interested in focusing my career activities in this industry. I am very much at home in soccer circles, and believe that peak performance comes from doing what you most enjoy.

After years of playing a key role in a successful family business, I'm ready to move on to a career situation that really capitalizes on my own major enthusiasms—and that brings me to your door. For your review, I'm enclosing a copy of my resumé.

I look forward to an opportunity to talk with you in the near future, and will call you early next week to see if we could arrange a time to meet.

Sincerely,

Alex Coughlin

Creating Your On-line Resumé

Although your on-line resumé may contain the same information as your paper one, it will have some key differences. Do the research required to assure you will be selected out of a company's database. Stay current with industry buzzwords, select key words carefully and show accomplishments and initiative.

Developing a Key-Word Section

Your resumé will be stored in a database from which information (resumés of likely candidates) will be extracted via a "query" based on key words. The best way to communicate your qualifications is to use key words and concepts that have an impact on the audience and trigger immediate interest in your product–you. The use of these words will ensure that your resumé is pulled out of the database that is being searched for specific skills or experience. The more key words your resumé contains, the greater likelihood that your resumé will be forwarded to a manager for consideration.

The following list will help you get started: however, it is not all-inclusive. After you have reviewed the following key words and concepts, circle the ones that apply to you. Use these in your resumé.

Technical and/or Managerial Skills Key Words

management/supervision

project management

budget development

recruiting

training

mediation

team building

territory development

strategic planning

problem definition analysis

systems development

systems administration

cost containment/ cost reduction

return on investment evaluation

quality orientation

continuous improvement

international operations

acquisitions/mergers

grant proposal development

concept-to-implementation project management

operations planning

change management

real estate financing

lead entry into markets

market definition

proven excellent judgment

strong operations/ administration experience

computer literate (Internet literate)

organizational ability

negotiating skills

research skills

verbal communication

public speaking presentations

Action Item

Read job descriptions carefully and develop a key word list targeted for the company to which you are sending your resumé. When posting a resumé to a generalized site, use your glossary or thesaurus to assure that you have included appropriate synonyms.

ASCII Text Resumé Format

An ASCII text resumé is a necessity for an on-line job search. It is relatively easy to create, if you have done your content homework well. Computers made it easy for candidates to create printed resumés that sometimes paid more attention to format than content, but when it comes to on-line resumés, the simpler the better. Two sample resumés follow. The first is an ASCII text resumé, and the second has the bells and whistles of a more traditional, graphically enhanced resumé: same content, different formats.

Your Name

Your Address

Your E-Mail/URL

Key Words

Put the key words up front because the text is searched from beginning to end, and the sooner the "hit" takes place, the more quickly your resumé will be identified as one that should be included.

EXPERIENCE

Current or most recent employers   Dates of employment

Title of your most recent position

A brief description of the situation in your current or most recent employment, for example, size of department, goal of unit, key products or some indication of magnitude.

ASCII Text Resumé

An ASCII text resumé can be "cut and pasted" into an e-mail document, eliminating the need to send it as an attachment.

Your Name

Your Address

Your E-Mail/URL

Key Words

Put the key words up front because the text is searched from beginning to end, and the sooner the "hit" takes place, the more quickly your resumé will be identified as one that should be included.

Experience

Current or most recent employers   *Dates of employment*

Title of your most recent position

A brief description of the situation in your current or most recent employment, for example, size of department, goal of unit, key products or some indication of magnitude.

Traditional Resumé

Food for Thought

> "It is good to have an end to journey towards; but it is the journey that matters, in the end."
>
> Ursula Le Guin
> American science fiction author
> 1929–

Scannable Resumé Format

The most common scanning device used for storing resumés into an electronic applicant tracking system is the Optical Character Reader (OCR). These machines are mixed blessings.

They get resumés stored where they can be accessed quickly, clear up the backlog experienced by the recruiting department, and level the playing field for everyone by minimizing the human factor in resumé review. They allow your resumé to be stored for longer periods of time and help your being considered for jobs you didn't know existed.

On the other hand, these readers can err, misreading the Y's on your resumé and turning them into V's or misinterpreting the typeface you selected, relegating your entire resumé to a collection of I's and O's. Machine readers might run the section headings into body text; they can stall at underlining, boldface type or poor contrast, turning your resumé into an indecipherable file.

David Bantam
RR 1 Box 20B
Alma, NE 68920
(308) 928-9013
bantamd@platte.unk.edu

EDUCATION
ioioioioioioioioioioioioioioioioioioioioioioioioioioioioioioioioio
ioioioioioioioioioioioioioioioioioioioioioioioioioioioioioioioioio

EXPERIENCE
ioioioioioioioioioioioioioioioioioioioioioioioioioioioioioioioioio
ioioioioioioioioioioioioioioioioioioioioioioioioioioioioioioioioio

COMPUTER SKILLS
ioioioioioioioioioioioioioioioioioioioioioioioioioioioioioioioioio
ioioioioioioioioioioioioioioioioioioioioioioioioioioioioioioioioio

Scanned Resumé
(Your resumé can turn into a collection of I's and O's.)

Your Name

Your Address

Your E-Mail/URL

Key Words

Put the key words up front because the text is searched from beginning to end. The sooner the "hit" takes place, the more quickly your resumé will be identified as one that should be included.

Experience

Current or most recent employers   Dates of employment

Title of your most recent position

A brief description of the situation in your current or most recent employment, for example, size of department, goal of unit, key products or some indication of magnitude.

List 3-4 accomplishments, in bulleted format. Bullets must be filled in and dark, because scanners tend to read hollow bullets or boxes as the letter "O."

Previous/Next most recent employer   Dates of employment

Title

Repeat the format above. This time, use only one or two accomplishments, unless you were in this position for several years and the most recent position was of shorter duration.

Education

List your degrees, training, or skills updates in this section. If your education is newly completed and it is your primary qualification for the job, move this section to follow **Key Words.**

Professional Affiliations/Achievements/Awards

Keep this section confined to the past three to five years (unless it was a Rhodes scholarship, presidential citation, Olympic medal or the like) and, for the most part, to job-related activities, organizations or awards. Your activities in the local chapter of the Basketweavers Guild need not be included, unless you are applying for a marketing manager position at a basket manufacturing company. The bonus you received for three years in a row as a result of your creative efforts for the United Way Loaned Executive program belongs here.

Scannable Resumé

If you want to be sure your resumé gets you into the database:

- Produce a version of your resumé that has no lines or boldface and that uses only upper-and lowercase characters. Avoid using shadowed or reversed typefaces. Yes, it looks plain vanilla. The thing is, the OCR likes plain vanilla.

- Use a standard type font such as Geneva, Arial, or Helvetica in the sans serif family. If you prefer a serif style type font, use Palatino, Times or New Century Schoolbook. You can mix fonts for effect but use no more than two fonts, or the resumé will take on a patchwork look. Don't condense spacing between letters.

- Use a font size between 9 and 14 points.

- Print your resumé on light colored paper (white is best, but pale gray or ivory may work). Use a laser printer for maximum contrast. High-textured paper is a risk at best, so use a good quality plain stationery stock.

- Be concise, yet use enough key words and phrases to define your skills, experience, education, and professional affiliations.

- For on-line help, visit Resumix's site at http://www.resumix.com/resumé-tips.html, where you'll find tips, a resumé builder form, and an excellent example.

Submitting Your On-Line Resumé

Some on-line job centers allow you to search and apply to several posted openings at the same time, to post your resumé for review by human resource personnel, and to read job postings from many organizations. Many companies have on-line forms for presenting your resumé. Make sure you *read the directions* and *practice* before you send or post yours. Avoid the temptation simply to sit down, identify openings or places to post your resumé, fill in the blanks and zap it off. Most of us write from two to twenty-two drafts of our resumé before we finally send it off in answer to an opportunity. When filling out an on-line resumé form, it is wise to download the form, develop your responses and then enter them on the form. Print and read the form, making sure it represents you well, that all the information is complete, and that there are no typos.

Eliminate anything from your resumé that may make it unreadable. For example, if you feel that you simply *must* show prospective employers a sample of the custom hats you design, develop a personal Web site and invite interested employers to visit you there. Make sure that you have noted this Web site's URL in your cover letter. Include in your resumé key words that describe your marketing skills, hat creation experience, and Web site design. Just do not try to include a graphic of the hat in an on-line resumé form.

On-Line Cover Letters

An on-line job search has some significant differences from a traditional paper-based job search when it comes to cover letters. Key differences in the on-line cover letter include the following:

- Many on-line resumé forms contain space for the cover letter to be an integral part of the document, so you won't create a separate letter. When this option is in the form, be sure to use it. An easy way to complete the cover letter portion is to cut and paste text from a word processed letter you have sent to other prospective employers. The good news: the form blanks let you paste in text from nearly any document. The bad news: many of these forms do not have a word wrap function, so that unless you enter hard returns at the end of each line, your document will run off the page. **Remember: read the directions first!**

- It will be more difficult to use the "compare experience to requirements" format for your cover letter, which is a very good way of making sure that your qualifications get noticed. The comparison is most often presented in a side-by-side table format. If you are using e-mail or a fill-in-the-blanks form, this will present a challenge. The best way to get around this problem is to use the paragraph header method. The following figure shows a sample cover letter that uses this method.

• Be sure to include a Key Word section in your resumé, because the database will be searched and matches made electronically. Read the job description carefully and make sure your letter and resumé contain some of those terms and phrases.

Lynn Jobseeker • 13344 SW Worry Free Lane • Miles Around, MN 33645

May 31, 2000

Gotrocks Company
PO Box 55443
Gotrocks, IL 61834

Attn: Human Resources

I am forwarding my resumé for your consideration for the Underwater Basketweaving Division Manager position as posted on your Web site. My skills and experience meet your requirements very well.

You require:

1. Excellent communication skills

2. Supervisory experience

My experience:

1. More than five years developing technical manuals and employee communications such as newsletters, benefits announcements, and instructional materials

2. Hands-on supervision of an employee relations department comprised of five HR specialists, three administrative employees, and two benefits coordinators

I will be happy to meet with you to discuss my salary requirements and the results I can bring to your Underwater Basketweaving Division.

Sincerely,

L. Jobseeker
lynnj@online.com
333-222-1111

Cover Letter with Paragraph Headers

Your Personal Cybercommercial

A personal cybercommercial is a concise statement that can be used to describe your experience and accomplishments in about 30 to 40 seconds (about as long as the average listener can stay focused) or that can be read in a few seconds. Most of the on-line resumé forms ask for such a statement. Develop yours and use it to introduce yourself in your in-person job search. Consider the following example:

> My name is Val Rosario. I have ten years of experience with increasing responsibility in sales management. As the leading salesperson for Xanadu Widgets nationally, I established a reputation for accountability and results with my national sales accounts. As a manager, I have developed five sales leaders in the manufacturing equipment industry. My strengths are developing talented people, selling, and marketing.

Presenting yourself in a positive way will be even more important during your on-line search campaign than the face-to-face campaign that is going on at the same time.

Sending Your Resumé or Other Information as Attachments

Your e-mail software will most likely allow you to send a document as an "attachment" along with your message, rather than including the entire document in the body of your e-mail. This is an extremely convenient tool—until you send something created in software that the receiving party doesn't have available, in which case the attachment won't be readable.

In job searching it's safest to assume that the other end does not have the same software. So ...

- If you are planning to send a complex document, ask the recipient if he or she can open files created in the program you are using. Be sure to specify the version as well.

- Enter your resumé in a site's on-line form and e-mail a request to clarify the programs in which work samples may be sent.

- Develop a Web site and post the information you would otherwise send as an attachment. Then you can refer to it in your resumé or e-mail.

- Cut and paste the information into an e-mail. Though you will very possibly lose much of the formatting, many e-mail software programs can accommodate at least basic formats such as italics or bullets.

Food for Thought

"Nine-tenths of wisdom consists in being wise in time."

Theodore Roosevelt
26th U.S. President
1858–1919

CHAPTER 7

Interview Preparation & Techniques

"Half the world is composed of people who have something to say and can't, and the other half who have nothing to say and keep on saying it."

Robert Frost
American poet
1874–1963

Research

Few job-seekers realize how important a little investigation can be prior to an interview. If you come into an interview armed with information about the company, you'll be able to ask intelligent questions and supply specifics about how you can benefit that company. It will also leave the impression that you are both savvy and willing to take initiative.

There are different ways to obtain useful information. If it's a large corporation, familiarize yourself with its products or services. Many corporations have brochures and publicity material available to the public. Use the reference desk of your public library to find articles that have been written in newspapers and magazines. For current financial information, try to obtain an annual report. This may also outline a company's goals for the next year.

Try to talk to an employee or former employee of the company. You can learn a lot from this person, but remember that what you're told may well be colored by his or her own (possibly negative) experiences.

Collect information that gives you a sense of the company's goals and identity, and that will prompt you to ask pertinent questions during the interview. These questions can cover everything from the background of the company to its plans for the coming years. These should always be general questions about the company, not ones that relate to you personally. Those will come later.

Your goal is to impress the interviewer with your questions and with the quality of your homework. You will have displayed your eagerness and shown that you're not just there to see what the company can offer you, but also how your skills and interests may benefit the company.

Food for Thought

> *"You cannot teach a man anything; you can only help him find it within himself."*
>
> Galileo
> Astonomer and Physicist
> 1564–1642

Answer these questions before your interview. The more you know, the better impression you'll make.

The basic information

• Interview—date and time: _____

• Interviewing for: _____

• Company: _____

• Phone: _____

• Address: _____

• Interviewer's name and position: _____

• Directions for finding: _____

Information that shows I know about the job

• Job description: _____

• The product or service: _____

• Skills required to do this work: _____

• Attitudes necessary to do this work: _____

• Results needed to be produced: _____

Information that shows I know about the company

• How long in business: _____

• Number of employees: _____

• Other branches: _____

• Company's customers: _____

• What does the advertising sell: _____

Competitors

• Is the company growing, staying the same, or losing business? Why?

_____

• Is the industry growing, staying the same, or losing business? Why?

_____

This sheet may be photocopied so you can use one for each interview.

Applications—More than Just Filling In the Blanks

Gather all the necessary information and learn to fill out an application that leads to interviews.

To an employer who has not met you, an application *is* you. An application that is filled out correctly can be impressive. It can help you stand out from the competition. It can draw attention to your skills and any results you have produced.

Take a look at the Employment History Summary Worksheet on page 130. Take time to fill it out correctly and in detail. Take it with you to use when you fill out applications. This will save you time and energy as well as show that you are well prepared and efficient.

When filling out an application:

1 Read and follow ALL instructions.

2 Be neat. Print legibly.

3 Use an erasable black pen or take white out with you to make corrections.

4 Complete all sections. Do NOT leave any item blank. If the question does not apply to you, write N/A in the appropriate space.

5 Avoid negatives. Examples: If you were fired from a job, write "terminated" as the reason for leaving the job. Add the phrase, "Please allow me to explain." Also add this phrase if you answer "no" to the question, "May we contact your previous supervisor."

6 In the special skills section of the application, emphasize skills and accomplishments. Include volunteer and special skills including software products and specialized machinery.

7 Take your Employment History Summary Worksheet with you to all interviews so that you will not forget any of this information.

Applications: Filling In the Blanks

Every application requires that you list past job duties. Usually the space for this information is very small. Write in the major duties, skills, or accomplishments from past jobs that you know are important for the job you are seeking.

Be Careful!

You need to be very careful with three questions on an application:

1 **Salary desired.** Put "open" in this blank.

2 **Willingness to relocate.** Use "open" here also.

3 **Position desired.** If you are applying for one specific position, write that position title in this block.

If you found in your research of the company several positions that interest you, include them. Do not write the word "*anything*" under position desired. This is a free ticket to the trash can.

You are answering these three questions in this way to get the interview. *Putting the wrong answers in these blocks may keep you from this goal.* You want to talk to the decision makers, show them the skills you have, and learn more about their needs. Only after you get the interview do the issues of salary, relocating, and position desired become important. You and the employer may find that you can work around these points if you are the right person for the job. This can only happen after you learn more about each other in an interview.

Food for Thought

> "We know what we are, but know not what we may be."
>
> William Shakespeare
> English dramatist and poet
> 1564–1616

References

Who knows you? Who is familiar with your skills and interests? Get the names, addresses, occupations, and phone numbers of three people who will be your references. The best references are employed people who are friends, former employers or co-workers, or people with whom you have done volunteer work. Do not list relatives unless requested.

Before you list your references:

 ### REFERENCE CHECKLIST

Check items when complete.

- ❑ Include your past supervisors. (Only if you know they will give you a good reference.)
- ❑ Ask permission before you use someone as a reference.
- ❑ Give a copy of your resumé to references. Ask for feedback.
- ❑ Review and remind them of projects you worked with them on.
- ❑ Confirm with them the reason you left the company.
- ❑ Let them know when someone may be calling them.
- ❑ Give them the name of the company so they will be sure to return the phone call.
- ❑ Ask them to let you know when they have been called.
- ❑ Follow up with them after the call to check information and get feedback.
- ❑ Let them know when you get a job.
- ❑ Keep in contact with people on your reference list.
- ❑ Maintain a good relationship with your immediate supervisor, so he or she can be included on your reference list.

By the time employers call your references, they are interested in you. A bad or incomplete reference can knock you right out of the running. If you have any doubts about a reference, choose another one.

Questions Often Asked in Reference Checks

- Can you verify the dates the employee worked for your company?
- What was the employee's job title?
- Can you give a basic description of the job the employee had?
- How would you rate the employee as a supervisor?
- How did the employee respond to supervision?
- Was the employee reliable and on time? Were sick days excessive or kept to a minimum?
- What was your working relationship with the employee?
- Are there any negative aspects of the employee that stand out?
- What positive attributes stand out?
- Can you verify the employee's salary?
- Is the employee eligible for rehire with your company?
- Did the employee receive raises or promotions while with your company?
- Did the employee display initiative?
- How did the employee interact with peers?
- What is your overall impression of the employee?

If the employee's former company has a strict policy regarding references, the questions will be limited to:

- Can you verify that (name) worked for your company?
- Can you verify his or her salary?
- Can you verify his or her dates of employment?

Employment History Summary Worksheet

(Make copies of this worksheet. Complete and take with you to interviews.)

Social Security Number: _____ Driver's License: _____

Organization Name: _____ Telephone: _____

Address: _____

Your Title(s): _____

Supervisor's Name: _____ Use as a Reference? Yes or No

Starting Month/Year: _____ Ending Month/Year: _____

Starting Pay: _____ Ending Pay: _____

Reason for Leaving: _____

Organization Name: _____ Telephone: _____

Address: _____

Your Title(s): _____

Supervisor's Name: _____ Use as a Reference? Yes or No

Starting Month/Year: _____ Ending Month/Year: _____

Starting Pay: _____ Ending Pay: _____

Reason for Leaving: _____

Organization Name: _____ Telephone: _____

Address: _____

Your Title(s): _____

Supervisor's Name: _____ Use as a Reference? Yes or No

Starting Month/Year: _____ Ending Month/Year: _____

Starting Pay: _____ Ending Pay: _____

Reason for Leaving: _____

Ready, Set, Interview

Become an expert on the company and the job for which you are interviewing. Learn how to make a good first impression.

Well, you did it. You got the interview. Now, all it will take is charm, right? The decision maker will ask the questions; you will answer them the best way you can…with your fingers crossed. Is there any more to it?

Yes, there's more. Lots more.

You can make this interview work for you. You can make yourself look great. All you have to do is get ready.

Prepare…Prepare…Prepare.

- Learn more about the company where you are applying and the position you want.

- Look closely at your skills, attitudes, and results produced. See how they match with what you have learned about the position and the company.

"How do I match up with what this company needs?" or "How can I be most useful to this employer?"

Let's look at the big three again:

- Skills

- Attitudes

- Results Produced

Skills

What skills are needed for this job? Do you have those skills? Where are you lacking? How can you overcome this lack? Which of the required skills are your strongest?

Prepare a new skills statement that is based on what this job requires. Using the new skills statement early in the interview can increase the interviewer's interest in you.

Get familiar with the required skills. During the interview, be sure to tell the employer about the skills you have—the ones needed for this job.

Attitudes

What sort of attitudes are required in the job you're applying for? What did you learn about required attitudes when you did your research? Which attitudes or qualities are you strong in?

Just as you prepared a new skills statement, now you can also prepare an attitude statement. With it you can clearly show an employer that you have what he or she needs.

Here are some statements that show valuable attitudes:

1 "I really **want to work.**" (Not, "I really need a job"–everyone needs a job. Employers want people who really want to work.)

2 "I'm always on time or early because I know time is money".

3 "I can be trusted to do my best to get the job done right."

4 "If I don't know how to do something, I'll ask."

5 "I want to work for a company where I can grow and advance."

6 "I believe I have a lot to offer an employer." (Be ready to back this up with skills, attitudes, and results you can offer.)

Statements like these are music to an employer's ears. If you show the right attitudes, you make hiring you less risky. The employer becomes more interested in you.

Results Produced

What does the employer want? Is there a backlog in the word processing department? A problem with quality in the parts produced on the assembly line? A decrease in sales?

What is needed to help make more money and improve the business?

This is hard information to find. And it is the most important. If you can't get it before the interview, you must get it during the interview.

In either case, you must think about results you have produced on other jobs. Have you helped to save time or money?

Did you come up with new ideas that worked? Did you increase sales? Decrease costs? Improve quality?

These don't need to be earthshaking. Sometimes small improvements, like rearranging a filing system, can help reduce the time needed to do filing. That means a worker has more time to do something else. That means increased profit for the employer.

Take time to write down the results you have produced on past jobs. Look at this list before you go to interview. Make sure you tell these things to the interviewer.

- As you gather information about the industry, company, job, and yourself, some questions will come up. Perhaps facts from one source do not agree with those from another source. Perhaps you simply need more information. Write down these questions and concerns. Bring that list to the interview.

- An employer will almost always ask, "Do you have any questions for us? That's the time to pull out your neatly written list, smile, and say "Well, as a matter of fact…"

- Is that impressive? You bet it is! The interviewer will see that you took time to learn about what the company needs. That is exactly the kind of worker who will be offered a job.

That Important First Impression

You did your research. You've looked over your notes on skills, attitudes, and results. As you approach the main entrance to the building, you feel those familiar butterflies in your stomach. The receptionist greets you and directs you to the boss.

Within five minutes, the interviewer will decide whether or not you are a likely choice for the job. How can this be?

Think about what you do when you meet someone new. You get a feeling or a first impression of that person. You can tell whether or not you're going to hit it off. It may not seem fair, but interviewers do the very same thing.

That important first impression comes from your:

> - Initial Greeting
> - Posture
> - Appearance/Clothing

Based upon these, the interviewer will decide whether or not you are likely to be right for the job. You will then be interviewed in a way that supports that decision. If the interviewer likes your look and feels comfortable with you, he or she will probably ask questions that bring out your strong points and reasons to hire you.

If you don't make a positive first impression, the interview probably will not go well. Remember this:

> **You only have one chance to make a good first impression.**

Relax. Fortunately, it's not that hard to develop some habits that will help you make a positive first impression. Let's look at how you can do this. Let's look at initial greeting, posture and appearance.

Initial Greeting

It's easy. All you have to do is:

- **Smile**
- **Make eye contact**
- **Offer a firm but gentle handshake**
- **Call the interviewer by name**

(If you don't know the name when you come into the building, ask the receptionist **before** you go in to the interview.)

Practice these four steps until they become natural.

Look in the mirror and see how you smile. Practice walking across a room, making eye contact, and extending your hand in greeting. Practice saying the interviewer's name correctly so that it feels familiar to you. This will help you feel less nervous. Feeling less nervous also helps with the first impression.

Why is eye contact so important? People who make eye contact are seen as trustworthy and likeable—qualities wanted in any employee.

Posture

Walk into your interview with your head up and your back straight. Think, "I am excited about being here. I am making this the best interview I can." Remember that you have something of value that this employer needs.

Try to seat yourself so that there is nothing between you and the interviewer. A desk, for instance, can become a block to easy communication. When you do sit down, take a moment to relax yourself:

- **Take a deep breath and let it out slowly and quietly**
- **Look around you**
- **Study the interviewer's office**

What do you see? Are there pictures, awards, diplomas, or other things that you feel comfortable commenting on? Do so as a first step, an "icebreaker," in meeting the interviewer.

Be relaxed in sitting, but don't slouch. Be aware of your body and what it is doing. Are you tapping your foot, wringing your hands, rubbing your nose? These are all signs of being nervous. You can control these.

Lean forward in your chair when you speak. Let that excitement come out. Nod your head and maintain eye contact as you listen to the interviewer. You should practice all of these at home or with your helping professional.

Appearance/Clothing

Hundreds of books have been written about what to wear to an interview. Take a look at a few of these at the library. Mostly, you need to know what is worn in the industry or company in which you want to work.

Visit places that hire people who do what you want to do. See how the employees dress. Notice the hair styles and whether there are beards, mustaches, or accessories like bracelets and earrings. Are the outfits sporty or conservative? Are men wearing suits? Are women wearing dresses or pants?

Each company has certain dress codes. Your interview outfit should match these standards and even be one step above them.

Practice for a Perfect First Impression

Practice can make those first five minutes successful

Put on your interview outfit. Get a friend to act the part of the interviewer. Walk into a room and do the four simple actions that make up the initial greeting.

Then practice sitting down and becoming aware of your body movements and posture. Look around. Focus on some object and use it as an icebreaker. Practice maintaining eye contact.

Do these until they all feel comfortable. And, best of all, when you walk into the real office for the real interview, you will feel that you have done it before. You'll make a great first impression.

We've been talking about doing research and practicing making a good first impression. An interviewer can't possibly know for sure whether or not you can do the job. Thus, he or she must use first impressions and make the best guess possible. The better the first impression, and the more you support that with your statements of your skills, attitudes, and results you've produced, the more likely you are to succeed.

Prepare. And practice. These both will result in better interviews. They also lead to more job offers.

Phone Interviewing

Most employers will contact you by phone to schedule an interview. Some may even conduct a "phone interview" with you to determine whether they would like to interview you in person. Your responses during the phone interview can be even more critical to getting the job than the personal one-on-one interview.

Here are some tips for phone interviews:

- DO answer the phone politely at ALL times during your job search. You never know who may be calling you and you want to make a good first impression.

- DO record a professional message on your answering machine or voice mailbox. Clearly state your name (or at least the phone number) and say you are unavailable but will return the call as soon as possible.

- DO let everyone in your household know you are expecting phone calls from potential employers. Ask them to answer the phone politely and take detailed messages if you are not available.

- DO return phone messages from potential employers as soon as possible.

- DO ask the caller to hold *briefly* while you gather your resumé, company information, and so on. Turn off the television or radio. Let household members know you are on an important call and ask them to keep background noise to a minimum.

- DO ask the caller if you can return the call at a better time, if necessary.

- DO treat the phone interview as a REAL interview. Respond to questions as you would in person.

- DO ask the interviewer what the "next step" is for a personal interview.

- DO NOT have small children answer the phone or take messages. You may not get the call or correct message.

- DO NOT eat during a phone interview. Chewing in someone's ear leaves a negative impression.

- DO NOT answer call waiting during a phone interview, unless you are expecting an important call. If this is the case, you may want to reschedule the conversation.

- DO NOT hang up first. Allow the caller to end the conversation to be sure that he/she has covered everything.

Food for Thought

> *"Speech is power, speech is to persuade, to convert, to compel."*
>
> Ralph Waldo Emmerson
> American essayist and poet
> 1803–1882

Panel Interviewing

Some employers interview in teams (two or more persons conducting the interview). Some of the reasons for this are:

- To save time

- To allow interviewers with different backgrounds to assess your qualifications

- To see how you interact with a group

- To see if you are at ease in a group setting

A panel interview should be treated the same as a one-on-one interview. Treat each person as important. Individuals who might appear to have no impact on the hiring decision may, in fact, be the most influential.

Here are some key things to keep in mind.

- Try not to be intimidated. Rarely do employers try to make you nervous.

- Breathe deeply and slowly.

- Greet each person with a handshake and a smile.

- Speak to everyone in the room. Make eye contact with each person from time to time.

- Ask at least one question of each person.

- Ask for everyone's name, correct spelling, and title.

- Send each person a thank you letter.

MIND OPENER

Conversation Is More than Words

When we talk, we communicate in three different ways:

1 **With our bodies.** This is what the listener sees. It is nonverbal communication like our clothes, posture, and facial expressions. These make up more than half of our total message. Even when we never open our mouths, we're still making statements of some kind.

2 **With our way of speaking—the delivery.** This is what the listener hears in our tone of voice, as well as how quickly we speak, how loudly, how high-or low-pitched the voice is. Eeyore in the book *Winnie The Pooh* is a great example. No matter what he said, he sounded depressed. The way you talk counts for about one-third of the total message.

3 **With our words.** These account for less than 10 percent of our total message. They are important, of course, but, if the listener doesn't like what he sees or hears, your actual words aren't going to change anything.

So, 90 percent of your message is in your nonverbal communication. It is in how you speak, rather than in what you say.

How can you get the right message across?

- **Use a video camera or mirror** to see yourself in action. What do your interview clothes, posture, gestures, and facial expressions say? Do you look shy, relaxed, nervous, too active?

- **Talk to a tape recorder.** This is good practice before using the phone, too. Your words and the way you speak are most of the message. Listen to your rate of peaking. Pay attention to the loudness and the tone of your voice. Do they change or are they too much the same? Is your voice uninteresting?

- **Role-play both telephone calls and face-to-face interviews** with positive and helpful friends. Show them this page. Ask for feedback.

Interviewers Can Throw Curves

Sometimes, those who are responsible for hiring employees ask difficult questions to learn how the interviewee will cope. For example, what if these questions were asked of you?

"Why do you want to work here?"

"What can you contribute?"

"Why should we hire you?"

Anticipating questions similar to the above and role-playing your answers with a friend (or in front of a mirror) are helpful. Practicing is a key to effective job interviewing preparation. Here are some tips.

- **Welcome all questions with a smile.** The moment you show irritation can be the moment you will be out of the competition. You can say: "That's a good question. I believe I have a good answer." The manner in which you answer questions is often as important as the answer you provide.

- **Give direct, honest answers.** You need not rush your answers, but try not to be indecisive. Indirect or awkward answers can cast a cloud over your credibility. Be straightforward. An honest answer, even if not perfect, will send a better signal than one that is vague.

- **Ask questions in return.** It is a good idea to go into each interview with prepared questions you want answered. An example might be:

  "When I do a good job, what opportunities will I have for additional experience?"

A potential employer has the right to reject you as an employee during your interview. You, also, have the right to withdraw from an interview, if you are not satisfied with the answers you receive.

Introduce the mutual reward idea. When the time is appropriate, indicate you understand that an ideal situation is when both the employer and employee benefit. You can get to the next step by discussing what you can do for the firm and asking directly what the organization can do for you.

Legalities

Discrimination against applicants on the basis of race, sex, age, or religion, is, of course, illegal. Most interviewers are well trained to avoid it, but it's useful to have some basic knowledge of what interviewers can legally ask you in case you suspect you're being interviewed unfairly.

Most applications state something like "Widget Corporation is an equal opportunity employer. We do not discriminate on the basis of sex, religion, color, race, age, national origin, physical handicap, or marital status."

The chances of being asked a blatant question about this type of information are low, *unless* the person interviewing you has never heard of the civil rights movement! But you may be asked questions in a roundabout way in order to expose information about one of these hands-off topics.

Many people aren't at all offended by "illegal" questions. In fact, they're proud to talk about their spouse, church affiliation, or the like, which is their right. However, all applicants have the option *not* to reveal this information.

Some companies are anxious to know personal information about you. For example, they may feel (rightly or wrongly) that married employees are desirable because they have settled down or that employees who belong to a church have a greater sense of morality.

Larger companies, especially those with government contracts, often have quotas to fill. This means that a certain percentage of their employees *must* be minorities and/or members of protected groups (over a certain age, war veterans, etc.). If you happen to be a member of a minority group, you may be looked upon as a more desirable candidate. However, you'll still need to have the necessary qualifications to be hired.

You should know that it's permissible for an employee to collect this kind of information as "post-hiring" data to be used for statistical purposes. Employers are encouraged to ask if you are willing to volunteer such information to help them comply with various state and federal requirements. You can volunteer the information when applying, or you can wait to see if you get hired and then answer the questions. The choice will be yours.

In the list that follows are areas in which illegal questions might be asked in your interview. Read through them now, so that you can think about how you would react. Will you answer everything? Challenge the interviewer? Will you say you don't feel the questions are pertinent to filling the job? Will you be offended? Think through what your response would be, if you were asked a direct question. Remember that such questions are generally not permissible and that you have the right not to supply the information.

The following areas of personal information are considered hands-off for employers making hiring decisions. This is not a complete listing of such areas. It is a sampling of some of the more general ones. State laws vary considerably on pre-employment discrimination laws. The laws that specifically prohibit discrimination are too long to list here.

- Questions regarding your marital status, number and/or age of children or dependents, provisions for child care, or your maiden name.

- Questions regarding pregnancy, childbearing, or birth control.

- Name or address of your spouse, closest relatives, or children (emergency information excepted).

- Questions that indicate with whom you reside.

- Questions concerning your race or color.

- Questions regarding your complexion or the color of your skin, eyes, or hair.

- Questions regarding your birthplace or that of your parents or spouse.

- Questions regarding your citizenship, nationality, or ancestry.*

- Questions about your height and weight.

- Requests that you attach a photograph of yourself to your application.

- Questions regarding your general medical condition.

- Questions regarding whether you have received Workers' Compensation.

- Questions regarding your religion or the religious holidays you observe.

- Questions concerned with whether or not you have a criminal record.

- Questions regarding refusal or cancellation of bonding.

- Questions regarding your military service (if any), including specific dates and type of discharge.

- Questions regarding foreign military service.

- Questions regarding your current or past assets, liabilities, or credit rating, including bankruptcy or garnishment.

- Requests that you list the organizations, clubs, societies, and lodges to which you belong.

*With the 1987 signing of the Immigration Bill, it is permissible to ask, "If you are not a U.S. citizen, do you have the right to work and remain in the United States?" You will be expected to provide proof of citizenship or documentation of your right to work, if hired.

MIND OPENER

This Body Isn't Perfect, But It's All I've Got. How Do I Talk about My Physical Abilities and Limitations?

In the interview, you can control how you present your physical abilities to an employer.

- Talk about what you can do—not what you can't.

- Make sure you can do all parts of the job you're seeking. Be able to explain this to an interviewer. Use examples.

- If you have a release from your doctor, bring it with you. This is a benefit to the employer. It's as if you have already had your pre-employment physical.

- Help the employer be specific about the parts of the job he or she thinks you may not be able to do. You can only correct a misunderstanding if you know what it is.

- Be able to talk about any hiring incentives that may be available to an employer who hires you.

- Remember, it's not just your physical abilities an employer needs. Your good attitude and your ability to get results are also important. Let the employer know about these.

Whatever your physical abilities are, you take them into your job. You cannot change them, but the job site can change to match them.

And Then There are the Gaps—the Times I Wasn't Working, What Do I Say about Those?

It's too late to change your work history, but you can present it in the best way possible.

1 **Be able to explain all the gaps.** Most people have very good reasons for them. Practice describing yours.

2 **If jobs ended for reasons you couldn't control (layoffs, plant closures), be able to explain them.**

3 If you made the choice to leave jobs, be able to explain why. Explain without "bad mouthing" the past employer.

4 If you gained skills or attitudes during your breaks in employment, be able to present these. We learn valuable lessons outside the workplace that are useful in the workplace.

5 To an employer, gaps mean that you might not stay long with a company or you may be undependable. Think about how long you will stay at a job before you go to the interview. What kind of time commitment are you willing to make?

Explaining Negative Situations

When you talk about past negative experiences, you may inadvertently display attitudes that will raise warning signals for your interviewer. You may harbor a negative attitude toward your former employer or supervisor, for example, but don't be *so* honest in an interview that you reveal all your pent-up bitterness or hostility.

Perhaps you and your former supervisor had a noticeable personality conflict that eventually led you to quit. If you say this, though, your interviewer may surmise that you are prone to interpersonal problems and be leery of hiring you even if your qualifications are rock solid.

Keep your explanations about negatives SHORT and quickly turn the focus of the conversation to what you have done to overcome the situation.

You need to be truthful about why you quit the job, yet at the same time you don't want to create an unfair strike against yourself in the process. What, then, is your best course of action? Give your side of the story in precise details, rather than in emotional generalities. Avoid vague comments like, "He (or she) just had it in for me from the start." Explain specific areas in which you and your supervisor disagreed and give examples of situations in which your ideas weren't used. You can describe how accessible you made yourself with no reciprocation from your supervisor, the accomplishments you had with little or no recognition, and so on. You need to give tangible and reasonable explanations for your leaving (or being laid off or terminated), without revealing your resentment. To sound truly mature and balanced, give the other side of the story as well. If you look beyond your hurt feelings, you may find the reasons your supervisor felt the way he or she did.

Explaining why you were terminated is rarely a comfortable process. Be candid while walking the fine line of not doing more damage to yourself as an applicant.

Some applicants have negative feelings not only towards their former employers, but towards the interviewer. If you're an attorney, you may feel it's ridiculous for the personnel manager to screen you before anyone in the legal department does. You may convey an attitude of indifference to the interviewer's evaluation because you assume that the personnel manager knows very little about the legal profession. Naturally, that person will be left with a negative impression, and your potential career with the company might already be over. Be sure to put all of your prejudices aside *before* your meeting.

Anxiety

Anxiety is another emotion that interferes with successful interviewing. We're not talking about nervousness. Interviewers see many good candidates who are nervous. The anxiety in this instance occurs when someone is literally overly anxious to land the job. Unemployed people, who are frightened by their situation, may say things like, "I'll do anything!" Rather than dedication, the interviewer may interpret this as desperation. This, in turn, may cause the interviewer to label you as lacking in motivation for the job in question.

If you truly *are* desperate and *will* do anything, at least make an attempt to carefully screen the jobs and companies you're looking at.

> **Tip**
>
> Consider applying for temporary, part-time work to support yourself while you search for a job tailor-made for you. Many great job offers have come out of temporary jobs.

To summarize, your interview will be directed by the person with whom you are meeting, since she'll know exactly what she wants to learn about you. It's essential that you tell her the truth about your background and that you explain negative events in an honest, balanced way. Prepare yourself to a reasonable extent. Expect to answer questions for which you're unprepared. Above all else, relax!

Before You Leave the Interview

Two important points:

- Make sure you get your questions answered so you can decide if the company is a good fit for you.

- Get business cards or complete names and addresses for everyone you interviewed with so you can send thank you letters.

SAMPLE QUESTIONS TO ASK THE INTERVIEWER

Review the list. Place a checkmark (✓) next to those that you want to take with you to your interview.

❏   What skills or experience do the superior performers exhibit?

❏   What results will be measured and how?

❏   What attitudes or personal qualities do you think an employee needs to fit in here?

❏   What are the next step(s) in your hiring process?

❏   How long have you worked here? Why do you stay?

❏   What would you like to see change about your job or the company?

❏   How are employees valued at this company?

❏   Others: _____

_____

_____

 INTERVIEW EXERCISE

You need a partner. Find a willing friend, spouse, or staff person and go where you will not be distracted. First, you will be the applicant and your partner the interviewer. Have your partner ask you some of the typical interview questions. Answer them as you would in an interview for a job that you really want. It's fun to tape record these role-playing sessions to help you learn. Do so, if you can.

During this role-play, you should ask the interviewer:

1 What skills or experience do you want in the person who takes this job?

2 What results will this worker be expected to produce?

3 What attitudes will this worker be expected to produce?

Have your partner give answers as if he were the decision maker at a company where you want to work.

After this, you can role-play the close. You should now:

1 Summarize two or three major parts of the job and show how you can do or learn them.

2 Ask the interviewer what required skills you may be lacking.

3 Ask what strengths he feels you could bring to the company.

4 State that you want to work for the company and why.

5 Ask when there will be a decision. Try for a specific time or date.

6 Thank the interviewer for the time spent.

After you have finished role-playing, think back to your answers (or play the tape). Were your answers:

- Positive?
- Brief, with action words and good examples?
- Related to the employer's needs?
- Easy to understand?

Now switch to playing the employer, and your partner the applicant. See how it feels to be the employer. How do your partner's answers make you feel?

MIND OPENER

How to Keep from Getting Hired

Look at the reasons some real employers give for not hiring. You can change these into positives for you just by doing the opposite.

For example, change:

"Lack of interest and enthusiasm" into *"Lots of interest and enthusiasm."*

"Fails to make eye contact" into *"Maintains eye contact."*

As you read the list, write down the opposite of each one on a separate sheet of paper. When you are done, you will have your list of "how to get hired!"

Reasons for Not Hiring

1. Has poor personal appearance.

2. Is overbearing or overaggressive, "Knows it all."

3. Is unable to express self clearly. Poor voice, grammar.

4. Lacks career planning. No goals.

5. Lacks interest and enthusiasm.

6. Lacks confidence. Nervous.

7. Interested only in best dollar offer.

8. Unwilling to start at bottom. Expects too much too soon.

9. Makes excuses or is evasive.

10. Lacks courtesy. Ill-mannered.

11. Lacks energy. Answers only "yes" or "no" to open-ended questions.

12. Speaks badly of past employers.

13. Fails to make eye contact.

14. Has limp, "dead fish" handshake.

15. Shows a lot of indecision.

16. Turned in sloppy application. Spaces left blank and scratch outs.

17. Wants job only for short time.

18. Has little sense of humor.

19. Lacks knowledge of industry, company, or job.

20. Shows no interest in company or industry.

21. Shows inability to take criticism.

22. Came late for interview.

Taken from *Realistic Return to Work* by Rick Lamplugh.

Negotiating Salary

Many people find this the most uncomfortable part of an interview, but it doesn't have to be that way. Just remember that this can be equally awkward for your interviewer, which means that you may be more emotionally in sync than you think.

Prepare for your interview with a few figures in mind: what you're currently making, what you would like to make; and the minimum you'll accept. While these aren't necessarily figures you'll end up agreeing on, they'll give you and the interviewer a base from which to work and serve to demonstrate how prepared you are.

Salary is one of the last things that should be discussed, and it's best brought up by the interviewer. If, early in the interview, you ask, "What does this job pay?" the answer may end up limiting you. A price will now have been named, and you won't have had the opportunity to show why you're worth more.

If, on the other hand, the interviewer asks, "What salary are you looking for?" or "Let's discuss remuneration," you will have a springboard from which to start. You can name a figure and emphasize the reasons why you feel you deserve that amount (without *over*-selling yourself or being completely immodest).

Unfortunately, you won't always have flexibility in negotiating salary. If you're a recent college graduate, you may not have a long salary history. Or you may be applying for a position in which the salary has little or no range. In situations such as these, you may have to decide whether you want the position enough to accept the figure offered. If instinct tells you there's no room for negotiation, don't push it.

Your research or prior history in a related job should give you an idea of what a given position should pay. Make sure you've done your homework, because it can be embarrassing to ask for a salary that's ridiculously higher (ten thousand or more) than the one being offered. Make sure you know what the market will bear.

Conversely, don't make the mistake of underevaluating yourself. Accepting a cut in pay will be expected, if you're changing careers and starting at the bottom. But if you're looking for a position similar to one you once had or have now, you should make every effort to *increase* your salary. Prospective employers look at salary history as a clue to your success in past positions. They'll make the natural judgment that you must have done well to get the promotions and increases you did. Salary history will also be used as a clue to personality traits such as aggressiveness and negotiating skills. Accepting significantly less money may work against you for all these reasons.

> ### Tip
>
> If you want a particular job so much that you're willing to take a cut in pay, you can try to make up the salary difference in other ways. Ask for three weeks of vacation rather than two, or negotiate a bonus system. Some people negotiate for overtime pay in positions where it wouldn't normally be paid or for "comp" days in exchange for overtime.

Interviewers assume that many applicants inflate their salary history. Misrepresentation isn't recommended, because prospective employers may go to great lengths to find out whether you've been truthful. If they think you're exaggerating, they may be less inclined to negotiate a higher salary for you. Once again, it's always prudent to be honest.

Negotiating Benefits

Like salary, you won't want to bring up benefits too early in the conversation. You may be perceived as someone who's far more interested in paid holidays than in the job itself.

The interviewer may broach the subject as he or she goes through an agenda of items to be discussed. If this is the case, you can integrate your questions into the conversation.

Be sure to ask more than simply whether medical benefits are offered. *Benefits* have come to mean a number of different things over the years. In their pursuit of hiring the best applicants, many companies have added more and more innovative benefits or "perks."

In today's competitive job market, the list can include:

- Medical insurance/HMO options
- Dental insurance
- Vision plan
- Prescription plan
- Life insurance/dependent life
- 401K plan
- Retirement/pension plan
- Profit sharing
- Paid holidays
- Vacation days
- Sick pay
- Long-and short-term disability
- Training programs (provided in-house or seminars that will be paid for)
- Tuition reimbursement
- Child care
- Employee exercise facility
- Van pooling
- Flextime
- Paid parking

Only the most innovative companies would offer all of these benefits to employees. Most offer only medical and life insurance, sick pay, and vacation days; other benefits are considered too expensive.

Applicants' needs and preferences in the area of benefits vary, depending upon lifestyles and priorities. The key is to know what your priorities are before an interview, so you can find out about those benefits that mean the most to you and your family.

Tip

Remember when you're discussing and negotiating benefits, ask who will *pay* for the benefits. Are they covered 100% by the employer? Is dependent coverage paid for? If the benefits are going to cost *you* too much, you may need to negotiate further.

INTERVIEWING DO'S (AND DON'TS) CHECKLIST

Trying to remember all the do's and don'ts, should's and shouldn'ts would be impossible. Refer to this list before each interview for quick reminders of the most vital things to remember. They have all been written in the positive *DO*, so just turn them around and you'll know the don'ts.

❏ DO research the position, company or field.

❏ DO practice interviews with a friend to ease your nervousness and pinpoint undesirable habits.

❏ DO ask for directions and parking instructions.

❏ DO give yourself ample time for the interview.

❏ DO try to arrange the interview when you won't have to worry about the time you're spending.

❏ DO confirm your appointment ahead of time.

❏ DO arrive alone, without bringing a friend or family member with you.

❏ DO arrive early.

❏ DO be prepared with names and addresses of references.

❏ DO prepare your references for receiving a call.

❏ DO take advantage of any and all contacts, including family members.

❏ DO use contacts to supply you with information.

❏ DO have ideas about salary before the meeting.

❏ DO overdress rather than underdress.

❏ DO treat the receptionist or secretary with respect.

❏ DO remember everyone's names and correct titles.

❏ DO complete the application or any forms given to you.

❏ DO make eye contact.

❏ DO give answers that are concise and relevant.

❏ DO ask questions of the interviewer.

❏ DO allow the interviewer to guide the conversation.

❏ DO tell the truth and exaggerate only if you can back it up.

❏ DO avoid pat and cliché-ridden answers.

❑ DO try to appear selective, even if you're overanxious.

❑ DO be prepared to discuss your former employers, even if the experience was negative.

❑ DO be prepared, if you're interviewing for a position where there's little room for salary negotiation.

❑ DO ask about specific benefits you're interested in.

❑ DO use benefits as a negotiating tool when possible.

❑ DO mention work experience and extracurricular activities while in college (especially recent graduates).

❑ DO follow up with a thank-you letter.

Most importantly, DO everything you can to appear and be relaxed!

 ## "WHAT TO TAKE TO THE INTERVIEW" CHECKLIST

The checklist below is to help you remember all the essential elements you'll need to take to the interview. This compilation will help you remember things that you might otherwise forget during this busy time.

❑ Copies of your resumé

❑ Copies of references list

❑ Notepad

❑ Erasable black ink pen

❑ Work history page (detail of the work history that is on the resumé)

❑ Copies of certifications, licenses, and so on

❑ Company information

❑ List of questions to ask the interviewer

❑ Directions to the company

Follow Up: Forget Me Not!

The interview is over. You say, "Boy, am I glad that's over." You can hardly wait to get home and relax. Now, all you have to do is sit back and wait.

Right?

Wrong.

Sitting back and waiting is what most job-seekers do. But you will be different. You will follow up on the interview.

> **Once an interview is over, two things occur:**
>
> • You begin to forget most of what happened.
>
> • The interviewer begins to forget most of what happened.
>
> *You must prevent this.*

Remember that positive impression you made? You want to continue to build on it. You also want to set yourself apart from the competition. There are three steps to take in doing this:

1 As soon as you leave the interview, do a self-evaluation.

2 Within 24 hours of the interview, send a thank-you note.

3 Make a later follow-up contact with the interviewer.

Let's look at how to do each of these.

Self-Evaluation

This takes only a few minutes and helps you remember the important parts of the interview. Do it right after you leave the interview. Don't wait until the next day.

It seems as if you won't forget a thing. But you will, and remembering is essential if you really want to get a job offer.

Doing a self-evaluation turns the interview into a learning tool. You become better at interviewing—a skill you will use for the rest of your life. Remember that every job change requires some kind of interview, and the average person changes jobs every two or three years.

Sharpening your interviewing skills will make job offers happen more quickly, now and in the future too.

 ## INTERVIEW SELF-EVALUATION CHECKLIST

- ❏ Did I do research on the company?
- ❏ How prepared did I feel?
- ❏ How did I handle the introduction?
- ❏ How effective were my experience stories?
- ❏ Did I ask enough/right questions?
- ❏ What questions did I not feel prepared to answer?
- ❏ How effective was the closing? (Do I know what the next steps are?)
- ❏ Do I know if they are seriously considering me? (Did I get a commitment?)
- ❏ What will I do diffently next time?
- ❏ Did I get the interviewer's full name, title, and address?
- ❏ What strengths do I want to highlight in my thank-you letter?
- ❏ Was I asked to provide any follow-up information?

The Thank-You Note

In many ways, this note is as important as the interview. When the interviewer has seen two, three, or seven applicants in a day, they start getting jumbled together in his or her mind. A thank-you note can set you apart from the competition.

Keep your note brief. Include these three main points:

1 A sincere "thank you" for the time the interviewer spent.

2 A mention of some topics that were discussed.

3 A brief restatement of your strong points in relation to the job.

Getting Back in Touch with the Interviewer

If you were able to arrange a specific time to make contact, be sure to do it. If you were not able to, then call three to five working days after the interview.

If you find that the position has already been filled or that you are no longer being considered for it, ask for a referral to another employer. The interviewer has spent time with you and has a sense of your skills and experience. He or she may know of another company that could use them. That referral could lead to a job offer.

Think about all that time and energy you put into reaching the interview. Your well-timed follow-up can help turn that interview into an offer. Or it can produce a referral to another employer. Either way, you win. You return to work and see paychecks come in.

Do Not Stop Your Job Search Until You Accept a Job Offer

So your interview went well. You expect to be offered the job. You expect to hear in a couple of days. Can you sit back and relax? First, ask yourself a couple of questions:

Does it make sense to wait for an offer that might not even come?

Does it make sense to watch days stretch into weeks and even months?

Of course not.

It's a temptation to quit this job search since it hasn't exactly been fun. But please don't quit. There are three very good reasons to keep at it:

1 Instead of losing valuable time by waiting, you may find, be offered, and accept another job. That means your paychecks come in that much sooner.

2 If you have another job offer, you can call the first employer with the news. Maybe then the first one will also make an offer.

3 It never hurts to have more than one job offer to choose from.

Food for Thought

> "No man has listened himself out of a job."
>
> Calvin Coolidge
> 30th U.S. President
> 1872–1933

CHAPTER 8

Looking Your Best

"A well-dressed man is he whose clothes you never notice."

W. Somerset Maugham
English author and master of fiction technique
1874–1965

First Impressions

Your mind will probably be racing as you anticipate what you'll say and how you'll behave, but the first impression you create will be visual and the importance of looking your best can't be overestimated.

When you research a company, you might learn that its policies are particularly conservative or that the prevailing attitude is extremely casual. *Whatever* you discover, a good rule of thumb is to overdress and lean toward the conservative. If it turns out that jeans and T-shirts are standard there, you can dress the part once you have the job.

Men should wear a suit and tie. The suit doesn't have to be dark, three-piece, or pin-striped, but it should be somewhat conservative in color and style. Naturally, there are situations where only a *very* conservative suit is appropriate, such as in interviews at financial institutions or law firms. On the other hand, if you're interviewing with a design or record company, it may be more suitable to interview in a sport jacket and trendy tie.

Women have more choices in dress and therefore can make more mistakes. Suits and conservative dresses are the best bet for women as well; avoid extremes in length, color, and frills. The more staid the company, the more conservative the outfit should be. You can personalize your clothes with tasteful, understated jewelry, and accessories. Stay away from pants, miniskirts, sweaters, and anything that's overly trendy or casual.

Tip

Interviews are an ideal time to make a mental note of how employees dress on the job, so that you'll be sure to look professional by dressing the part when you are—hopefully—an employee yourself.

Communicating Your Best Image

Dress for Success!

There is a direct connection between your appearance and your self-confidence. The better your self-image when you arrive for an interview, the more positive your attitude will be.

To help you prepare, some specific grooming areas are presented below. Combined they constitute the physical image you will communicate. Rate yourself in each area by circling the appropriate number. A 5 indicates no further improvement is possible. A 3 or lower indicates improvement is needed. Be honest! Most job-seekers have difficulty seeing improvements that can be made.

 ## APPEARANCE ASSESSMENT

		High				Low
1.	Hairstyle, hair grooming (neat/clean)	5	4	3	2	1
2.	Personal hygiene (clean fingernails, etc.)	5	4	3	2	1
3.	Cleanliness of clothing (pressed?)	5	4	3	2	1
4.	Appropriate shoes (clean, polished?)	5	4	3	2	1
5.	Choice of clothing (conservative?)	5	4	3	2	1
6.	Choice of clothing (appropriate for the work environment you seek?)	5	4	3	2	1
7.	Accessories (not too wild)	5	4	3	2	1
8.	**General statement:** Once you are ready to an interview and you look in the mirror, you make a statement. Is it what you really want to look like?	5	4	3	2	1

If you rated yourself less than 3 in any area, improvement should be your first order of business. Ask someone you trust to evaluate how you look in your job-seeking outfit, then make necessary adjustments. Maintain the same standard in all interviews.

Look Your Best for Any Job

Hair: Clean, combed, trimmed, and cut to industry standards.

Makeup, perfume, aftershave: Avoid overuse. You want the interviewer to think about your skills, not your eye shadow or overpowering aftershave.

Fingernails: Trimmed and clean. Avoid long nails and bright polish.

Shoes: Clean and shined and without holes or defects.

Is There a Basic Outfit?

Yes, there is. The basic outfit is for jobs that require "work clothes" or uniforms and have little public contact (mills, factories, kitchen help, etc.):

Men	Women
Shirt: Solid colored or lightly pin-striped. Don't roll up the sleeves. No flannel shirts.	Conservative dress or blouse and skirt. Avoid low-cut tops or short skirts and dresses.
Slacks: Gray, blue, or brown, dress type. No jeans.	**Pantsuit:** Conservative and businesslike; not sporty.
Belt: Avoid oversized belts and buckles.	**Accessories:** Avoid distracting ones like oversized earrings, six or seven rings, eight bracelets.
Socks: Solid color that blends with pants and shirts.	
Ties: Optional, but in most cases it will make you look even better.	

What Is an Image Outfit?

The image outfit is worn in office settings or to jobs with public contact (offices, restaurants, sales, etc.):

Men	Women
Dress up the basic outfit with:	*Dress up the basic outfit with:*
Conservative sports jacket or blazer.	Matching jacket for your blouse and skirt combination.
Solid or striped tie that accents your outfit. If you can't tie one, learn now or buy a clip-on tie and learn later.	Avoid wearing a pantsuit.

Food for Thought

"What is success? I think it is a mixture of having a flair for the thing that you are doing; knowing that it is not enough, that you have got to have hard work and a certain sense of purpose."

Margaret Thatcher
British Prime Minister
1925-

CHAPTER 9

Skill Upgrading

"An investment in knowledge always pays the best interest."

Benjamin Franklin
American statesman, scientist, inventor, and author
1706–1790

Maintaining and Upgrading Your Skills

Those who find themselves in-between jobs are in an ideal position to upgrade their skills. Here's why:

- When you improve your skills (whatever they may be), you immediately improve your marketability.

- Taking a course in one's area of specialization is an excellent way to balance the time you spend on job-hunting with something that can rejuvenate your attitude.

- Mixing with others in your field of expertise provides networking opportunities.

At first, it may seem strange that skill upgrading should be a part of a serious job search. Most people might say to themselves: "I've already got my skills, all I need to do is find someone who can benefit from them." This is true; however, skills change and a new, prospective employer may not be satisfied with your previous level of competency.

In her previous job as a receptionist/word processing operator in a small dental clinic, Emily had often wished that her English skills were better. When her husband was transferred to a new community 200 miles away, she decided it was time to upgrade her English and letter-writing skills. Emily enrolled in a Community College program for one semester. Near the end of the term, one of her new friends and classmates mentioned that her company was interviewing. With the renewed confidence upgrading her skills gave her, Emily landed a job much better than the one she had left. In addition, her training had simplified her job search.

CHAPTER 10

Utilizing Support Services

"Experience is a hard teacher because she gives the test first, the lesson afterward."

Vernon Saunders Law
Pittsburgh Pirates pitcher
1930

Making Your Search a Team Effort

Support services—college placement bureaus, State Human Resource departments, private employment agencies—often play a significant role in a job search. The recommended attitude is to view such agencies as "partners" who will guide and encourage you through the job-finding process.

Interviews with professionals who provide such services at all job levels indicate that some job applicants fail to take full advantage of the services provided. Here are mistakes they often make:

- Failure to make the best possible impression on agency personnel who have the responsibility of setting up interviews.

- Failure to fully accept counseling and guidance provided.

- Failure to make their best efforts in following through on interview opportunities.

- Failure to do adequate research about the firm where an opportunity exists.

Many people find it impossible to find a suitable job on their own, yet they do not take full advantage of the support services available. Three steps are recommended.

1 Make a list of those support services available in your community. Your local public library and community college can provide such a list.

2 Treat these support services as though they were employers who might use your services. Dress up for interviews, get their reaction to your resumé, and seek and accept advice.

3 Make a major effort to build one or more important relationships with personnel at each support service. Get them on your job search "team" and make sure it winds up as a mutually rewarding experience.

CHAPTER 11

Creating Your Own Job

"But now all I need in order to have a future, is to design a future I can manage to get inside of."

Francine Julian Clark
"Eligible Impulses" in a Wider Giving

Creating Your Own Job!

Over 90 percent of those people reading this book seek employment from a corporation or government agency. It is what they have prepared themselves to do. It is what they want. It is the way it should be.

But a small percentage may not react well to the necessary restraints connected with being on someone else's payroll. They have the entrepreneurial spirit deep within themselves, and eventually it will surface. Some of these individuals knock themselves out trying to find employment with others, when the opportunity to create their own job is staring them in the face.

> Susan spent almost six months searching for a job as a graphics specialist (her college major) without success. One afternoon, while being interviewed by the owner of a small business, he replied: "We really can't afford you as a full-time employee, but we would be interested in some contract work with you." Today, two years later, Susan has her own graphic design shop with two employees of her own.

Opportunities for people to create their own jobs has never been better.

- More large and small firms are discovering that it is profitable to contract all forms of work to others.

- The cottage industry mentioned by Alvin Toffler years ago is growing. For example, people who do telemarketing for large firms often operate out of their own homes.

- All you need to do is observe the many small trucks and vans in a community to realize that many with craft skills (home repairs, rug cleaning, landscaping) are in business for themselves.

Depending upon what you have prepared yourself to do, creating your own job may not be as farfetched as you may have thought.

CHAPTER 12

Goals:
Self-Discipline

"Without discipline, there's no life at all."

Katharine Hepburn
American Actress
1907–

Realistic Job-Finding Goals

In a tight and tough labor market, having a life goal is great. *But it is not enough!* You need to supplement your life goal with short, practical, day-by-day job-getting goals. Without them, you begin to drift. Time gets away from you.

Listed below are some possible short-term goals if you can devote full days to your job search. If you intend to search while holding down a full- or part-time job, adjustments can be made. If you accept the goals as printed, place a check (✓) in the appropriate box. If you do not, make whatever adjustment you wish in the spaces provided.

JOB-FINDING EXERCISE

		Agree	Adjustments
Goal 1:	Find and win the best job available within 90 days.	☐	_____ _____ _____
Goal 2:	Find, and go through with, from one to three interviews per week.	☐	_____ _____ _____
Goal 3:	Devote an average of four hours per day (weekdays) searching for and keeping interviews.	☐	_____ _____ _____ _____

You may object to setting a 90-day limitation on a job search because it often takes longer. True. But the 90-day period is only a *goal*. The sooner you expect to find the right job, the sooner it may happen.

The truth is that if you intend to find a job *your way*, you must set your own goals to fit your own style. Even if you change them later, start off with realistic goals that fit the type of search you will be making. When you reach a goal, no matter how small, give yourself a reward.

MIND OPENER

Job Possibility Thinking

Been looking a long time? Getting discouraged? Maybe it's time to look wider and deeper. Maybe it's time to take a look at different kinds of jobs. In other words, maybe you can increase your number of job goals.

This step can be a hard one. Not only do you have to let go of seeing yourself in your old job, you have to come up with new ideas. Let's give it a try.

Robert Schuller describes 10 commandments of possibility thinking in his book, *Tough Times Never Last But Tough People Do*. Seven of them are printed here along with some of my ideas that relate them to your job search.

1 **Never reject a possibility because you see something wrong with it.** No job is perfect. Separate the negatives from the positives. Build on the positives.

2 **Never reject an idea because it's impossible.** Almost every great idea was first seen as impossible. What's more important is whether this "impossible" job would be good for you. If it is, go after it.

3 **Never reject a possibility because your mind is already made up.** No one is perfect. Remember that the human mind is like an umbrella. It functions best when open.

4 **Never reject a possibility because you don't have the money, manpower, muscle, or months to achieve it.** Instead, commit yourself to going after that job. Clearly identify what you need to achieve it. Then ask for help.

5 **Never reject a possibility because it's not your way of doing things.** Plan to adjust. If you could still do what you are used to doing, you'd be doing it. You *can* learn new ways of doing things and seeing yourself.

6 **Never reject a possibility because it might fail.** There is risk in everything. Identify problem areas, and then figure out how to fix or avoid them.

7 **Never reject a possibility because it's sure to succeed and you're not sure you can handle it.** This is not the time to be humble. Use this time to improve yourself. After that, you can help others.

APPENDIX A

Measure Your Progress

"I am always ready to learn, but I do not always like being taught."

Winston Churchill
British Prime Minister
1874–1965

Measure Your Progress

Completing a Second Profile

Now that you have completed the book, you are ready to do a second profile to match with your first. Please follow these rules:

- Study the profile form on the next page.

- Keep in mind that you know more about the job-search process than when you did your first profile, but, as yet, you may have not put any of the suggestions into practice. This means you are still rating what you anticipate and expect to accomplish, not your actual performance.

- A score of 8, 9 or 10 means you are ready in a given area and no further preparation is necessary.

- A score of 5, 6 or 7 indicates you understand what is required in a category but you are not fully prepared. Further reading, study, and practice are still necessary for success.

- A score of 1, 2, 3 or 4 is a strong signal you are not ready in these areas. Considerable reading, study, and practice are recommended.

- Compare your post-profile with your pre-profile. Identify those areas where progress has been made. Indicate weak areas where you feel additional preparation is necessary.

CONSTRUCT YOUR PROFILE FOR THE SECOND TIME

Categories	1	2	3	4	5	6	7	8	9	10	11	12

Column labels: Attitude, Prospecting, Professional Networking, Telephone Skills, Internet & Electronic Search, Resumé Preparation, Interview Preparation & Techniques, Looking Your Best, Skill Upgrading, Utilizing Support Services, Creating Your Own Job, Goals: Self-Discipline

Vertical axis: 10 9 8 7 6 5 4 3 2 1 0

Interpreting Your Profile

Study your profile carefully to discover your strengths and weaknesses. If possible, compare it with the profile of another individual and discuss the difference. Fieldtesting shows that almost everyone has three or more weak areas. Those who have had little or no job-hunting experience often show six or seven categories under a score of five. The more high categories you show on your profile, the more personal confidence you should have when you start your search.

You are encouraged to tally your numbers in each of the 12 categories to measure your "readiness" to begin a professional jobhunt. If you have been completely honest with yourself, the figures can be interpreted as follows.

- A score from 100 to 120 is a signal that you are in an excellent position to undertake the challenge. If you follow through in each area, you should eventually win one of the best jobs for which you qualify in the geographical area you have chosen for yourself.

- A score of 70 to 100 indicates you are in a good position to start your search but would save time and improve your possibilities by upgrading your weak areas.

- A total point score of under 70 is a strong signal that you have considerable work before you are ready to start a serious job search.

It is important to recognize that each job search is as different as the individual making it. Sometimes very high scores in a few areas (image, resumés, attitude) may compensate for low scores in other areas (networking, skill upgrading, interview preparation). The professional approach, however, is to be above average in all categories and excellent in as many as possible.

After you recognize and accept your weak areas, you are encouraged to weigh one category against the other according your master strategy. To do this, prioritize the 12 categories by placing the number 1 under what you feel to be the most important, 2 under the next important and so on down the line until what you feel is the least important of all is assigned 12. Obviously, top priority areas deserve greater attention, especially if you gave them a low score.

To help you fully understand the implications (dangers) of not improving your weak areas, see the suggestions under each category starting on the next page.

Checking Out Your Lower Scores

Naturally, the more strong categories shown on your profile, the better prepared you are to conduct a professional job search. Fieldtesting shows, however, that almost everyone has a few weak areas. Find out what lower scores (7 or under) can mean by reading under the appropriate headings below.

Attitude

If you have a negative attitude toward the job-finding process, you have a big problem that can be overcome *only* if you change your attitude. One thing that might help is to start thinking of finding a job as a game that should be played every day. The key to success is to keep expecting to get a job until you get one. This takes a positive, positive attitude! Sometimes you may need to back away from the hunt for a few days now and then so you can rebuild your positive attitude.

Prospecting

Fieldtesting shows that many individuals do not fully understand the concept of prospecting and do not accept the idea that more time must usually be spent finding good interviews than anything else. In a sense, you become your own employment agency when you seek a job. You must prospect in all directions at the same time. One or two irons in the fire are not enough.

Networking

Networking should start *before* you leave a job, not after. If you have neglected or have been haphazard about building relationships with key people in your career area, start today. Make a list. Talk to these people. Ask their advice. If possible, attend meetings or conventions where you can meet people who are influential. Too many applicants rely on resumés and newspaper want ads to gain interviews. In a tough labor market, such activities are only a start. Networking, properly done, produces the best result.

Telephone Skills

A weak rating in this category could indicate you have a psychological block in using the telephone to sell yourself. If so, read a good book on telemarketing techniques; select the opening introduction you intend to use; practice on your own telephone-answering device. Many people agree that it is easier to set up an interview by telephone than it is to appear in person and then have to return at a later date. Sitting around an employment office, waiting to see if you can get an interview, is often a waste of time. Save time, transportation costs, and wind up with more and better interview opportunities by using a telephone.

Internet & Electronic Search

The Internet can uncover another hidden job market. Being weak in this area will continue to limit your options and access to valuable information. Knowledge of how to use the Internet is also a skill that employers will value. Ignoring developing your knowledge and skills in this area will put you at a disadvantage in your job search and options.

Resumé Preparation

There is a saying among professionals that if a resumé is worth doing, it is worth doing right. A poorly prepared resumé may not produce the desired result, which is winning an interview with the person who can hire you. A low score is a signal that the applicant should seek professional help.

Interview Preparation and Techniques

Most applicants are weak in this area. They are either overconfident and feel they can "talk their way into a job;" or they are too lazy to do a professional job of preparation. An applicant who has not taken time to learn as much as possible about the firm he would like to join, is usually wasting time about going through the interview process. How can you ask intelligent questions about a career with a firm if you have no information to go on? Most organizations interview many candidates for a single job opening. To stay competitive, preparation is necessary.

If you figure you are weak on interview techniques, remember that all of us learn from experience. Every time you go through an interview, critique yourself. Did you ask too many questions? Did you leave knowing you wanted the job; whether you got it or not? If nothing else, ask a friend to act as an employer so you can go through a mock interview to get the feel of it. What you say, the way you look, and whether or not you communicate a positive attitude toward hard work will all supplement your resumé and put you into the final lap of the race.

Looking Your Best

A low score in this category indicates one of two things. First, the individual may have a poor image and needs to make improvements, or second, the person is underestimating the importance of making a good first impression. Different interviewers read different things into grooming. When an individual makes a sloppy appearance, an interviewer may conclude that the person might not be an organized, quality producer.

Skill Upgrading

A low score in this category might mean that the individual should be involved in taking one or more skill-training programs *while* a job search continues. Experts who frequently survey the labor market claim that the demand for skilled people usually remains high even in a tight labor market. Skill upgrading should be continuous for both the employed and the unemployed.

Utilizing Support Services

If you rated yourself low in this area, you are lucky because, compared to other job-finding activities, getting help from support agencies is easy. Start out by making full use of your state Human Resource Agency. Become involved in any activities they recommend. Investigate placement centers on any college campus near you—whether you have ever attended the college or not. Look into a private employment agency. You may wind up paying half of your first month's salary should they place you in a job that meets your desires; but, in the long run, the help you receive could be worth the price. In working with a support service, check them out thoroughly and if you determine they are credible, *accept their advice and follow their suggestions.*

Creating Your Own Job

If you rated yourself low in this area, you may not have any interest in being a contract worker, or a consultant or to work out of your home. If so, exploring further might be a waste of your time. If, however, you have overlooked the possibility of working for yourself, you have a whole new world of possibilities to explore. Go to your local library and start out by looking at books with titles similar to *Working For Yourself.*

Goals: Self-Discipline

Rating yourself low in this category is an admission that you need help. First, you need help in goal-setting techniques so you can organize yourself for a serious job search. Second, you need help in selecting daily, weekly, and monthly goals that will help you discipline yourself to spend so many hours job-searching each day. Finding and winning a good full-time job can be a difficult full-time job in itself. Until you "get real" and start following the 12 steps, you may just "hang out" and do little but spin your wheels.

APPENDIX B

Sample Resumé Sections

Your Contact Information

Function:

- To make your identity immediately and explicitly clear.

- To make it easy for the employer to contact you.

Key Items for Inclusion:

- Your name

- Your street address, city, state, and zip code

- Your home phone number, including the area code

Optional Item for Inclusion:

- Your work or message phone number. This is especially important, if you do not have an answering machine on your home phone.

Additional Points:

- Consider using a slightly larger typeface for your name and bold print for visual emphasis.

- Repeat your name at the top of the second page of a two-page resumé.

Statement Of Your Career Objective

Function:

- To ensure that your resumé is a well-focused, tightly integrated sales tool, rather than a miscellaneous summary of distracting autobiographical data.

- To provide the criterion for inclusion and exclusion, emphasis and de-emphasis of everything else that follows.

- To be the "drive shaft" in drafting and editing the body of your resumé.

Key Items for Inclusion:

- Cite functional area of expertise and interest, as in department sponsoring the contributing role.

  For example: Corporate Finance

- Give generic focus, so it will include related jobs.

  For example: Human Resource Development

- Consider using a specific job title when you are a strongly qualified candidate for an available position.

  For example: Senior Training Specialist

- Be concise, eliminating personal agendas like "a challenging, meaningful position ... leading to advancement to management" and rambling hype such as "with compensation commensurate with contribution."

Optional Items for Inclusion:

- Cite your functional area of expertise and interest, and related contributing roles you could play.

  For example: "Business Information Systems," "Systems Analysis," "Office Automation," "Programming," "Computer Education."

- Cite the level of responsibility you are seeking, if it is key to the assessment of your candidacy.

  For example: "Entry Level," "Supervisory" or "Senior Staff."

- Cite the industry you have targeted, if you have narrowed your objective to this degree.

  For example: "Health Care," "Computer Industry" or "CPA Firm."

- Include one or more mission statements, showing your understanding of the core functions and purposes of the work you are seeking, crucial factors to the success of your awareness of key priorities.

  For example: "Occupational Nurse: Consultation, Education, and Treatment for Wellness in the Workplace."

Food for Thought

> *"If we could sell our experiences for what they cost us, we'd all be millionaires."*
>
> Abigail Van Buren
> American Newspaper Columnist/Lecturer
> 1918-

Examples of Career Objective

OBJECTIVE

Auditing Position / CPA Firm

OBJECTIVE

Sales Representative / Nutritional Products

OBJECTIVE

Product Support

• End-User Documentation • Customer Training

OBJECTIVE

Assistant Manager Trainee

• Management Support • Efficient Operations • Strong Customer Service

---

OBJECTIVE

Entry Level Position / Advertising

• Product Promotion Strategies and Campaigns • Positioning for Visability
• Building Personality

OBJECTIVE

Management Position / University Admissions and Records

• Systems and Procedures for Timely Processing of Applications
• Collaborative Relationships with Faculty
• Service-Oriented Dealings with Prospective and Current Students and Alumni

---

Summary of Your Qualifications

Function:

- To create a bridge between your objective and the rest of your resumé.

- To be a power-packed summary of formal and informal qualifications for your objective.

- To capture attention and create receptivity to the detailed information that follows.

- To frame yourself in terms of how you wish to be seen, beyond the obvious facts of your experience.

Key Items for Inclusion:

- Cite number of years of experience.

- Cite type of experience, such as "direct," "related," "diversified," "increasingly more responsible," "business," "contributed services," "avocational," "intern," etc.

- Cite key skills and tasks that contribute themes in your qualifying experience and that support your objective.

- Cite specialized studies, if applicable, referencing details later in the Education category.

Optional Item for Inclusion:

- Cite relevant attitudes and personality traits that contribute to your superior performance. *For example:*

For a Production Inspector:

- Commitment to carefully checking details to support product quality.

For a Plant Security Officer:

- Strong safety-consciousness, vigilance in maintaining readiness for emergencies, and promptness in responding to calls.

For a Training Specialist:

- A leader in managing change and providing personal support in adapting to related stresses and challenges.

Additional Point:

- It is often easier to write your Summary after you complete the other sections of your draft. At that point you can extrapolate key selling points about yourself as a "lead" into the body of your resumé.

Examples of Summary of Qualifications

OBJECTIVE

Tax Internship

QUALIFIED BY

Specialized studies, a sudent leadership position using organizing, communication, and promotional skills, and work experience in meeting deadlines, doing bookkeeping, and providing client services.

OBJECTIVE

Marketing Professional

QUALIFIED BY

Three years of direct, diversified and increasingly responsible experience in developing marketing strategy, and conducting and managing campaigns for corporate communications and product promotion.

OBJECTIVE

Telecommunications Analyst

QUALIFIED BY

Specialized professional studies, and nine years of corporate experience in assessing needs, designing cost-effective methods and procedures, troubleshooting and solving workplace problems, and training employees in the use of technical products.

OBJECTIVE

Program Manager / Operations

QUALIFIED BY

Twenty-four years of varied decision-making experience with proficiency in managing multiple demands and pressured conditions. A lengthy track record of accountability in producing targeted results, backed by extensive engineering and business studies.

Listing of Your Key Skills

Function:

- To showcase your strongest relevant abilities—elements clearly applicable or transferable to your career objective.

- To establish yourself as a person who can add value—proficient, capable, and effective in specific, defined ways.

- To serve as a guide in filtering your experience for the most relevant supporting accomplishments to present.

- To validate accomplishments from other spheres as relevant because of the transferable skills you displayed.

Key Items for Inclusion:

- Cite the functional skills you do best and enjoy most—natural knacks that lend themselves to effective performance in the work you seek to do and/or;

- Cite your technical skills and special knowledge, which establishes your formal expertise in your field.

Additional Points:

- Analyze your objective for key skills underlying successful performance; then thoroughly review your background for matching skills.

- Sort out your primary from your secondary skills, relevant from irrelevant skills, and untangle overlapping categories.

- Narrow your list to a manageable number, selecting between two and ten key skills or areas of effectiveness.

- Refine the titles of your skills as needed.

- Present your skills in columns or clustered phrases, set off by bullets for emphasis.

Note: A listing of your key skills is highly recommended. It is not always necessary to include this as a discrete section. A strong *Qualified By* statement may be sufficient to showcase your skills. Whether the *Key Skills* section warrants development is a judgment call.

Factors affecting your decision include your particular skill base, as it relates to your objective, and space constraints in the presentation of other information.

Examples of Key Skills

KEY SKILLS

• Assessing • Organizing • Implementing • Streamlining

KEY SKILLS

• Consulting • Decision Making • Coordinating
• Troubleshooting • Expediting

AREAS OF EFFECTIVENESS

• Event Coordination	• Multimedia Presentations	• Customer Relations
• Promotions	• Copywriting and Editing	• Direct Sales

AREAS OF EFFECTIVENESS

• Feasibility Studies, Cost Estimates, and Proposals
• Client Presentations and Consultation
• Project and Program Management

AREAS OF EFFECTIVENESS

• Direct Nursing Care
• Health Eduacation Counseling, Information and Referral
• Employee Evaluation/Job Assignment and Modification
• Records Management and Payment Processing

AREAS OF EFFECTIVENESS

• Cultural Services	• Public Relations
• Community Development	• Fund Raising

AREAS OF EFFECTIVENESS

• Systems and Procedures Development	• Data Processing Support
• Work Simplification	• Document Control

Profile of Your Related Experience

Function:

- To establish core reference points of your qualifying experience in objective, factual terms.

- To provide employers with a clear framework for understanding you professionally and comparing you with other applicants.

- To provide a basis for third party comment on the skills, responsibilities, and achievements recommending you for hiring.

The Strategic Handling of Your Experience

- *To optimize your experience* involves a series of creative judgment calls on how to sequence, highlight, and de-emphasize various facts of your background.

- *Uncompromising honesty* is the bottom line for all representations you make about yourself. And, as any marketing professional can tell you, within the bounds of honesty, you have tremendous freedom to make the most of what you have to offer.

- A precondition to having others see the applicability of what you have done to what you want to do is *your ability to see yourself in that light*. As you approach the strategic handling of your experience, this guide provides you support on several major points:

   A. Issues Regarding Inclusion, Emphasis and Perspective

   B. Treatment of Your Core Reference Information

   C. Treatment of Your Description

   D. Treatment of Your Experience in Each Resumé Format

A. Issues Regarding Inclusion, Emphasis and Perspective

Type of Experience You May Cite:

- Experience from every realm of your life may be cited, clustered in groups under subtitled headings referring to the nature of the experience.

- Showcase your strongest categories of experience by sequencing them first, regardless of how recent or informal they were. *For example:*

Career-Related Employment	Internships	Consulting Contract
or		or
Other Business Background	Employment	Contributed Services

- Consider using header statements to strengthen weak or unrelated experience. *For example:*

Part-time and Temporary Jobs Financing Higher Education

Kinds of Jobs to Cite:

You only need to include professional jobs. Your resumé is not a company application form, requiring you to list all employment you have held. It is a targeted sales tool, presenting a full accounting of all *relevant* positions.

For example, if you have had a well-established career, been laid off in a downsizing, and needed to do temporary interim work outside of your field at a lower level of responsibility and pay, you are not required to include this information on your resumé. Measures taken to stabilize yourself financially, while searching for an appropriate position, are personal, adaptive responses to necessity. They should not dilute your candidacy and bargaining strength for a new career position.

On the other hand, if support positions have been your sole experience, or the bulk of it, over a substantial period, cite them on your resumé. Delineate your employment history in terms of the most challenging responsibilities you have handled and use these accomplishments as a bridge to career advancement.

When to Start Your Record of Experience:

Start your record of experience whenever you want. Leave the burden of initiative on the employer to probe back further if he or she wishes. However, once you begin your professional track record, you may not delete a full-time regular position simply because it did not work out, without becoming subject to a charge of fraudulent misrepresentation and risking later dismissal.

Food for Thought

"Everybody gets so much information all day long that they lose their common sense."

Gertrude Stein
American author and patron of the arts
1874–1946

B. Treatment of Your Core Reference Information

Core reference information includes the skeletal facts of your employment history—positions you have held; employers you have worked for; where they are located and when you worked there.

Formula:

Title, Organization, Location by City and State (Dates by Years Only)

Title:

- Use exact titles, if they clearly recommend your hiring.

- Use equivalent titles, if your exact title might be biasing.

- Use a function, if your title or series of titles would undermine your candidacy.

- Your title is frequently the most relevant and helpful information to emphasize, highlighting your level of responsibility and/or expertise. You will usually want to capitalize on it. In contrast, you will usually want to treat the name of the organization you have left, or are seeking to leave, without visual emphasis.

Organization, Location by City and State:

- Cite these explicitly. They represent keystones of the resumé's credibility to an employer.

- A subset phrase directly underneath the core reference information may be used to clarify the nature and size of operation of the employer. Typically a one-liner and no longer than three lines, it is chiefly relevant for established managers in portraying the context of personal achievement.

Dates by Years Only:

- Give an accurate, though approximate, chronology. Leave the burden of the initiative on the employer to probe for more exact dates.

- De-emphasize any gaps in months of service, keeping the focus on your skills, knowledge, and accomplishments related to your objective.

- Put dates at the end of the Title, Organization, Location line, or after description, to de-emphasize significance. Consider putting dates in parentheses to further visually de-emphasize them.

Format Options for Core Reference Information:

When you have had one major departmental affiliation per major employer:

Title, Organization 1, Location by City and State *(Dates by Years Only)*

Title, Organization 2, Location by City and State *(Dates by Years Only)*

Title, Organization 3, Location by City and State *((Dates by Years Only)*

Title, Organization 4, Location by City and State *(Dates by Years Only)*

When you want to trace your progression within one or more organizations:

- Organization 1, Location by City and State

  First Title *(Dates by Years Only)*

  Second Title *(Dates by Years Only)*

- Organization 2, Location by City and State

  First Title *(Dates by Years Only)*

  Second Title *(Dates by Years Only)*

- Organization 3, Location by City and State

  First Title *(Dates by Years Only)*

Additional Points:

- Cite your present or most recent job first, working backward. Exception: delineating subclusters of experience where entries fall in chronological order under the referenced headings.

- Single space entries to minimize prominence of the nature or number of jobs you have had; otherwise, when space permits, double-space entries.

Examples of Core Reference Information

EXPERIENCE

DEPARTMENT MANAGER TRAINEE, Filene's, Braintree, MA	(1992–Present)
BUYER, Jordan Marsh, Hanover, MA	(1990–1991)
ASSISTANT MANAGER, Connally's Children's Wear, Quincy, MA	(1988–1989)
ASSISTANT BUYER, Bradlee's Hingham, MA	(1986–1987)

EXPERIENCE

ACCOUNTING MANAGER, Audio Futures, Atlanta, GA   (1986–Present)
Electronic sound equipment manufacturer. Sales $6 million; 65 employees.

CONTROLLER, Optima, Inc., Savannah, GA   (1982–1985)
Fine art retailer/wholesaler. Sales $8 million; 38 employees.

ACCOUNTANT, Industrial Glass, Miami, FL   (1979–1982)
National glass manufacturer/wholesaler. 200 employees in corporate office.

EXPERIENCE

Career Related Positions:

CLIENT SERVICE ASSOCIATE, Pillips-Hill, Inc., Denver, CO	(1986–1988)
SALES MANAGER, United Parcel Service, Boulder, CO	(1981–1985)
ASSISTANT SALES MANAGER, Leemy (W.A.) Ltd., Logos, Nigeria	(1978–1980)

Employment Financing Graduate Studies:

DIRECTOR OF SECURITY, Captain's Cove, Inc., Provo, UT	(1991–Present)

EXPERIENCE

Hewlett Packard, Palo Alto, CA

SUPERVISOR, GENERAL STORES & PURCHASING	(1983–Present)
SUPERVISOR, MATERIAL CONTROL	(1976–1982)
RELATED SUPPORT POSITIONS	(1968–1975)

C. Treatment of Your Description

The description information identifies your relevant record of direct or related experience. Ground your selling points in concrete accomplishments. "For instances" that demonstrate effective performance should predict your contribution and success with a new employer.

Formula:

Did what, with, or for whom, on what scale, with what results.

- *Did:* identifies the skill, consequently using the past tense that can assume present usage

- *What:* describes the task

- *With Whom:* notes colleagues or clients/customers addressed

- *For Whom:* includes contextual reference such as department, type of business, industry

- *On What Scale:* describes, in objective terms, where possible quantifying achievement–size, speed, cost, percentage, number of people, time frame, etc.

- *With What Results:* define the purpose, explicit benefits, established impact–turnaround accomplished, new business developed, liability limited, efficiency improved, volume of business expanded, etc.

Additional Points:

- Start your accomplishment statements using power-packed action verbs. Lead with the strongest words you can, to emphasize your skilled contribution.

- Avoid using the personal pronoun "I" or the possessive pronoun "my." This will keep the tone objective, crisp, and professional.

- Avoid using subjective self-evaluation through adjectives like "creative," "intelligent," and "enterprising." Use strongly worded accomplishment statements so that the employer can deduce such things about you.

- Cite contextual reference of settings that are different from what you are now targeting in generic terms that will enhance transferability. For example, describe a church as a service organization.

- Discuss your experience in terms meaningful to your target audience. For example, a retiring military officer might focus on logistics and personnel management rather than the specifics of weapons systems. Avoid specialized jargon.

Examples of Accomplishment-Oriented Description

Coordinated six fund-raisers benefiting the American Heart Association, including bike-a-thons, candy sales, and door-to-door drives. Recruited and supervised volunteers of up to 100 people, and raised over $5,000.

Earned all personal living expenses during four-year course of undergraduate study by maintenance of full-time service employment.

Fielded up to 20 customer service phone calls per day, troubleshooting problems, cutting red tape, and making special arrangements as needed to maintain good will relationship and stimulate repeat business for a retail travel agency.

Determined process bottlenecks in three production units of a heavy industrial and agricultural chemical manufacturer. Instituted process modifications that increased production by 20 percent and reduced labor and raw material costs by 30 percent.

Served as the primary provider in Quality Assurance of SPC on torque of critical fasteners, bringing enhanced ability to pinpoint faulty parts, failing tools, and ineffective areas of production processes.

Conducted a production inventory and calculated costs as a consultant to a specialty retail store; findings led to shift in purchasing strategy.

Redesigned structure and established key functional areas and committee for a tennis club, which resulted in a 33 percent increase in membership.

Planned the catering, set design, and marketing for 10 real estate broker open houses to promote client properties, with an attendance of 200+ each.

D. Treatment of Your Experience in Each Resumé Format

"Experience" in the Chronological Resumé

You can enliven the traditional, historical format. Replace the mundane, abstract, and or overly detailed description often found in chronological resumés with selective, persuasive examples of relevant accomplishments.

Formula:

- Reference core information for a particular job.
- Follow this with a brief illustrative narrative, emphasizing personal accomplishment.
- Repeat the sequence for each job experience.

Title, organization 1, location by city and state *(Dates by years only)*

Description–Did what with or for whom, on what scale, with what results.

Title, organization 2, location by city and state *(Dates by years only)*

Description–Did what with or for whom, on what scale, with what results.

Title, organization 3, location by city and state *(Dates by years only)*

Description–Did what with or for whom, on what scale, with what results.

Additional Points:

- You may want to make a brief statement about the nature and scope of your personal responsibilities as a context for subsequent bulleted accomplishments, highlighting your personal excellence and contribution in the job.

- Each experience you cite can take the form of a responsibility summary with modifying accomplishments, or a like summary of one or more freestanding accomplishments. Treatment can vary on the same resumé from reference to reference.

"Experience" in the Functional Resumé

You can present the core structure of your experience in immediate satisfaction of an employer's need for the "big picture" of your background, while elaborating on your related track record. The format should minimize any marketability issues and accent your contribution and success.

Formula:

- List core reference information job-by-job, under the heading Experience.
- Do not include other elaborating information in this section.

Title, Organization 1, location by city and state *(Dates by years only)*

Title, Organization 2, location by city and state *(Dates by years only)*

Title, Organization 3, location by city and state *(Dates by years only)*

Descriptions are contained under a separate category with the heading *"Related Accomplishments."*

- "Did what with or for whom, on what scale, with what results" provides the structure for writing your accomplishments.

- Your Related Accomplishments may come from any arena of your life experience, as long as you have a reference point somewhere on your resumé.

- Be selective in what you cite, showcasing only your most senior and relevant experience. This means that many elements of a particular job may not be cited; whole jobs may not merit description; and some part-time, brief, unpaid, avocational, and other such experience may be given status.

- As explicitly as possible, link your selected "for instances" to your Key Skills.

- Ensure that all of your Key Skills appear in your Related Accomplishments.

- Do not be concerned about having a separate Related Accomplishment for every Key Skill cited. In some cases, a Related Accomplishment will illustrate two or more of your Key Skills. This may occur one or more times.

- When clearcut parallels can be established, match the sequencing of your Related Accomplishments to the sequencing of your Key Skills.

Profile of Your Related Education

Function:

To establish credit and noncredit credentials, completed or in progress, that testify to your relevant knowledge base.

Key Items for Inclusion:

- Degrees completed or in progress–Variations on status of degree:

    Level of degree, *Focus of Degree*, Year of completion

    Level of degree, *Focus of Degree*–In Progress.
    Completion: x Semester, 2000

    Level of degree, *Focus of Degree*–In Progress. x units or
    x percent completed

    Level of degree, *Focus of Degree*–Studies in Progress

Second Line of Information:

Degree-granting institution, location by city and state

Additional Points:

- Cite your most recent degree in progress or completed, then work backward in time.

- Delete any reference to an associate degree when a bachelor degree is completed.

- Delete any reference to high school diploma when an associate degree is completed.

- Visually emphasize the focus of the degree, rather than the degree-granting institution. Exception: when the degree-granting institution is so prestigious that citing it is a major leveraging factor.

- Delete the focus of your undergraduate degree, if it varies from your present objective, or if it may bias your target audience. *For example:* when targeting business jobs, do not focus on Elementary Education, Theology, etc.

Optional Items for Inclusion:

- Additional categories, or further delineation of degrees, such as:

    Honors and Awards; Leadership Positions; Professional Development Seminars; Employer-Sponsored Training; Certificates; Licensing Status; Related Course Work.

Examples of Education

EDUCATION

GRADUATE, Albany High School, Albany, GA

Employer-Sponsored Training: Dale Carnegie Course

EDUCATION

Three years of coursework leading to a Bachelor of Arts degree
Rutgers University, New Brunswick, NJ

Master Electrician, State of New Jersey

Employer-Sponsored Training:

Management/Supervision
- Certificate in Management
- Manufacturing Supervision
- Meeting Leadership
- Communication Skills:
  Assertiveness; Business Writing

Technical
- Management Overview of Robotics
- Cincinnati Milacron Robotics
  Operations
- SQ-0 Microprocessor Welder Control
- Programmable Controller Operations:
  Allen-Bradley; Gould Modicon;
  SQ-0 881

EDUCATION

BA, 1990, Loyola University, Chicago, IL

Leadership Positions:
Award-winning Public Speaker; Captain of Tennis Team;
Community Council Representative

EDUCATION

MBA, Finance, 1989, Suffolk University, Boston, MA

Earned while working full-time. GPA 3.84
Coursework Emphases: Economic Forecasting and Capital Budgeting

BA, Psychology, 1979, Boston College, Chestnut Hill, MA

Citation of Your Related Memberships

Function:

- To carry your professional identity full circle:

  –from establishing your focus in the Objective

  –to distilling your major selling points in the Qualified By section

  –to profiling your power-packed Key Skills

  –to direct or related Experience and Education descriptions

  –through relevant professional affiliations

- To create a subliminal identification of "I am one of you," in touch with the state-of-the-art developments and key issues in the field, etc.

- To support access to colleagues who can be helpful to you in your networking initiatives.

Key Items for Inclusion:

- National and local professional groups in your functional and/or industry interest areas.

- *The Encyclopedia of Professional Associations,* readily available in libraries, is a good source for national groups. You can join local chapters of national groups at moderate fees, which may be tax deductible.

- Networking is a good source of information on local professional organizations, which are often cohesive, informative and vital groups of significant value.

- List any offices held or major service roles performed for professional groups in which you have been active.

- List any honors or awards bestowed upon you for distinctive performance in your profession.

Examples of Membership

MEMBERSHIP

International Association of Business Comunications

MEMBERSHIP

• American Marketing Association   • National Transportation Society

MEMBERSHIP

American Bankers Association
Program Chair, Continuing Education Division

MEMBERSHIP

American Socety for Training and Development

Winner of Chapter Award for Innovative Leadership, 1992
Community Service Committee Member

MEMBERSHIP

Institute of Electrical And Electronics Engineers

Conferece Presentation:
"Evolution of 19mm Magnetic Tape Standards for Video,
Instrumentation and Data Processing"
Tenth IEEE Symposium on Mass Storage

MEMBERSHIP

Data Processing Management Association

Elected Leadership Positions:
Board of Directors (1988-Present); Vice President (1990-1991);
Secretary (1991-1992)

Afterword

MAPPING YOUR CAREER is an adaptation of materials developed by Cuyahoga Community College for their job-readiness program. The objective of the program is to prepare graduating students for the job search process.

The original workbooks and instructor guides were produced under the direction of Career Place, a unit within the Workforce and Economic Development Division of the College. Collaborating with Crisp Publications provided the college access to developed and proven content that was tailored to address 80% of what any job seeker needs to know. Consequently, MAPPING YOUR CAREER is applicable for learners of all ages and job seekers at various levels of experience and academic accomplishment.

Roadmap to Your Future, the genesis for this book, is the result of a collaborative effort by the following employees and partners of Career Place:

Managing Editor/Project Manager: Kathy Telban

Content Contributors: Patty Flauto, Linda Woodard

Editor: Mary Louise Rogers

Graphic Consultant: Shelly Meadows

Graphic Researcher: Marguerite Schmitter

Marketing Consultant: Beth Schumaker

Program Theme Conception: Wendall C. Garth Sr., Colette Taddy Hart, Greg Klayber, Elizabeth Okwudi, Crystal Stokes, Kathy Telban

Reviewers: Vondell Petry, Colette Taddy Hart, Suzanne Walsh, Linda Woodard

Cuyahoga Community College is Ohio's first, and largest community college serving 55,000 students each year at four campuses. For more information about CCC or the *Roadmap to Your Future* program, contact Career Place at 216-987-3029, or www.career-place.cc.

CAREERS, EDUCATION & JOBS

Crisp publishes a number of different kinds of books that can be resources for career planning and job-hunting. A few of them are listed here but many more can be found on our Web site, CrispLearning.com

Find The Bathrooms First
Roy J. Blitzer & Jacquie Reynolds-Rush

A fresh look at what people think and do immediately after taking a new job. This is a career-building book that will help in today's job market. 1-56052-553-3

Designing Creative Resumés
Gregg Berryman

Originally created for writers and designers, it also serves as a guide to creative presentation and encourages the reader to demonstrate initiative and imagination. 1-56052-053-1

jobsearch.net
Carrie Straub

Marketing skills effectively in cyberspace is a new component of job-hunting. 1-56052-451-0

Be True to Your Future
Elwood N. Chapman

The principles of developing life scripts to better understand and prepare for changes in education, jobs, and career—and a positive approach to life planning. 0-931961-47-5

Designing Creative Portfolios
Greg Berryman

Portfolios present varied materials and samples of work showing the range and variety of an individual's work. Contains step-by-step instructions. 1-56052-113-9

FIFTY-MINUTE™ BOOKS

Successful Career & Life Planning
Stephen G. Haines

Stephen Haines feels that everyone should create a strategic plan, and use it as a tool to manage their lives. 1-56052-562-2

Finding Your Purpose
Barbara J. Braham

Discover insights about how people think and behave and find purpose. 1-56052-072-8

Creating Your Skills Portfolio
Carrie Straub

A quick way to collect memorable work and projects to show others. 1-56052-394-8

Successful Lifelong Learning, Revised (previously The Adult Learner)
Robert Steinbach

This book shows how to develop a strategy for lifelong learning that includes the interests and needs of worklife and personal expression. 1-56052-563-0

Preparing for Your Interview
Diane Berk

A practical primer for the job-hunter—develops successful interview techniques and provides tips on how to avoid common interview-related mistakes. 1-56052-033-7